More Praise for Progress

'His unfailing optimism and well-argued points generate powerful good-news vibes.'

Esquire

'An exhilarating book. With the combination of arresting stories and striking data, *Progress* will change your understanding about where we've come from and where we may be heading.'

Steven Pinker, author of *The Better Angels of Our Nature*

'Johan Norberg chronicles the still largely unknown fact that humanity is now healthier, happier, cleaner, cleverer, freer and more peaceful than ever before. He also explains why in this superb book.'

Matt Ridley, author of *The Evolution of Everything*

'At a time of profound pessimism, Johan Norberg is refreshingly, but not glibly, optimistic. His excellent book documents the dramatic improvements in people's lives and reminds us of the huge potential for further progress – provided we are open to it.'

Philippe Legrain, author of *European Spring*

'In this brightly written, upbeat book, the Swedish author blends facts, anecdotes, and official statistics to describe "humanity's triumph" in achieving the present unparalleled level of global living standards . . . While acknowledging the mayhem, hunger, and poverty still facing much of the world, the author remains optimistic that human ingenuity will prevail in shaping the future. A refreshingly rosy assessment of how far many of us have come from the days when life was uniformly nasty, brutish, and short.'

Kirkus

'Excellent…Norberg's book comprehensively documents the myriad ways the state of humanity has vastly improved over the past couple of centuries.'

Reason

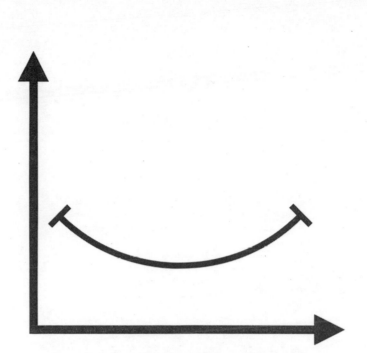

PROGRESS

Ten Reasons to Look Forward to the Future

JOHAN NORBERG

ONEWORLD

A Oneworld Book

Published by Oneworld Publications 2016
This updated paperback edition published 2017
Reprinted, 2017

Copyright © Johan Norberg 2016, 2017

The moral right of Johan Norberg to be identified as the
Author of this work has been asserted by him in accordance
with the Copyright, Designs and Patents Act 1988

ISBN 978-1-78607-065-4
ISBN 978-1-78607-232-0 (ebook)

Typeset by Hewer Text UK Ltd, Edinburgh
Printed and bound in Great Britain by Clays Ltd, St Ives plc

Oneworld Publications
10 Bloomsbury Street
London WC1B 3SR
UK

Stay up to date with the latest books,
special offers, and exclusive content from
Oneworld with our monthly newsletter

Sign up on our website
oneworld-publications.com

FSC
www.fsc.org
MIX
Paper from
responsible sources
FSC® C018072

To Alicia, Alexander and Nils-Erik – it's your world now.

[T]he Progress of human Knowledge will be rapid, and Discoveries made of which we have at present no Conception. I begin to be almost sorry I was born so soon, since I cannot have the Happiness of knowing what will be known 100 Years hence.

Benjamin Franklin, 1783

CONTENTS

Introduction: The good old days are now   1

1 Food   7
2 Sanitation   31
3 Life expectancy   41
4 Poverty   63
5 Violence   83
6 The environment   107
7 Literacy   129
8 Freedom   139
9 Equality   161
10 The next generation   189
Epilogue: So why are you still not convinced?   205

Notes   219
Acknowledgements   239
Index   241

Introduction

THE GOOD OLD DAYS ARE NOW

Nothing is more responsible for the good old days than a bad memory.

Franklin Pierce Adams[1]

Terrorism. ISIS. War in Syria and Ukraine. Crime, murder, mass shootings. Famines, floods, pandemics. Global warming. Stagnation, inequality, refugees.

'Doom and gloom, everywhere', as a woman on the street responded when public radio asked her to describe the state of the world.[2] It seems to be the story of our time.

These perceptions feed the fear and nostalgia on which populists of the Right and the Left campaign. Donald Trump's presidential campaign slogan made the case that America had to become great *again*, like it was in the good old days. Fifty-eight per cent of those who voted for Britain to leave the EU in the country's recent referendum say life is worse today than thirty years ago.

In 1955, thirteen per cent of the Swedish public thought

that there were 'intolerable conditions' in society. After half a century of expanded human liberties, rising incomes, reduction in poverty and improved health care, more than half of all Swedes thought so.[3]

Many experts and authorities agree. General Martin Dempsey, chairman of the Joint Chiefs of Staff, recently testified before US Congress: 'I will personally attest to the fact that . . . [the world] is more dangerous than it has ever been.'[4] Pope Francis claims that globalization has condemned many people to starve: 'It is true that in absolute terms the world's wealth has grown, but inequality and poverty have arisen.'[5]

On the political left, activist Naomi Klein argues our civilization is 'on a collision course', and that we are 'destabilising our planet's life support system'.[6] On the right, philosopher John Gray thinks that human beings are 'homo rapiens', a predatory and destructive species that is approaching the end of civilization.[7]

I used to share their pessimism. When I began to shape my worldview in Sweden in the 1980s, I found modern civilization hard to stomach. Factories, highways and supermarkets to me were a dismal sight, and modern working life seemed sheer drudgery. I associated this new global consumer culture with the problems of poverty and conflict that television brought into our living room. Instead, I dreamed of a society that put the clock back, a society that lived in harmony with nature. I hadn't thought about the way people had actually lived before the Industrial Revolution, without medicines and antibiotics, safe water, sufficient food, electricity or sanitary systems. Instead I had thought of it more in terms of a modern excursion into the countryside.

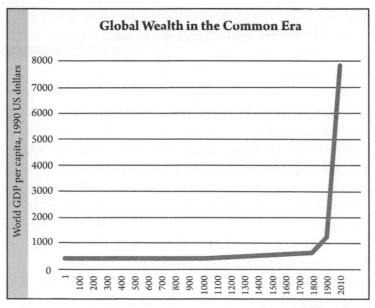

Source: Maddison 2003.[8]

But I started reading history and travelling the world. I found I could no longer romanticize the good old days once I began to understand what they had really been like. One of the countries on which I focused my studies experienced chronic undernourishment – it was poorer, with shorter life expectancy and higher child mortality than the average sub-Saharan African country. That country was my ancestors' Sweden, 150 years ago. The truth is that the good old days were awful.

Despite what we hear on the news and from many authorities, the great story of our era is that we are witnessing the greatest improvement in global living standards ever to take place. Poverty, malnutrition, illiteracy, child labour and infant mortality are falling faster than at any other time in human history. Life expectancy at birth has increased more than twice as much in the last century as it did in the previous 200,000 years. The risk that any individual will be exposed to war, die in a natural disaster, or be subjected to dictatorship has become smaller than in any other epoch. A child born today is more likely to reach retirement age than his forebears were to live to their fifth birthday.

War, crime, disasters and poverty are painfully real, and during the last decade global media has made us aware of them in a new way – live on screen, every day, around the clock – but despite this ubiquity, these are problems that have always existed, partially hidden from view. The difference now is that they are rapidly declining. What we see now are the exceptions, where once they would have been the rule.

This progress started with the intellectual Enlightenment of the seventeenth and eighteenth centuries, when we began to examine the world with the tools of empiricism, rather than being content with authorities, traditions and superstition. Its political corollary, classical liberalism, began to liberate people from the shackles of heredity, authoritarianism and serfdom. Following hot on its heels was the Industrial Revolution of the nineteenth century, when the industrial power at our disposal multiplied, and we began to conquer poverty and hunger. These successive revolutions were enough to liberate a large part of humanity from the harsh living conditions it had always lived under. With late twentieth-century globalization, as these technologies and free-doms began to spread to the rest of the world, this was repeated on a larger scale and at a faster pace than ever before.

Humans are not always rational or benevolent, but in general they want to improve their lives and the lives of their families, and with a tolerable degree of freedom they will work hard to make this happen. Step by step, this adds to humanity's store of knowledge and wealth. In this era, more people are allowed to experiment with different perspectives and solutions to problems than before. So we constantly accumulate more knowledge and every individual can contribute and achieve on the shoulders of hundreds of millions who have come before in a virtuous cycle.

This book is about humanity's triumphs. But it is not a message of complacency. It is written partly as a warning. It would be a terrible mistake to take this progress for granted. There are forces at work in the world that would destroy the pillars of this development – the individual freedoms, open economy and technological progress. Terrorists and dictators do what they can to undermine open societies, but there are also threats from within our societies. Nationalist and authoritarian politicians want to dismantle individual freedoms and start building walls between countries again.

These forces want us to think that the world is dangerous and that things are spiralling out of control, because frightened people think differently. Social psychologists who study authoritarian attitudes make the case that they are not based on a stable personality trait, but on a predisposition that can be activated under certain circumstances. When people think that their society or their group is under threat they begin to express more authoritarian and protectionist views even on issues that are not related to the particular threat. It's a flight from freedom, and into something supposedly familiar, safe and secure.

Frightened people do not ask for opportunities, but for protection. They don't vote for openness and freedom, but for the strongman who promises them security and provides easily identifiable scapegoats. If we think we don't have anything to lose in doing so, it's because we have a bad memory.

It is precisely for this reason that we have to remember that when people are allowed freedom, they don't create chaos, but progress. At this point in time we have to study the amazing accomplishments that resulted from the slow, steady, spontaneous development of millions of people who were given the freedom to improve their own lives, and in doing so improved the world. It is a kind of progress that no leader or institution or government can impose from the top down.

This book is about this progress, about what happened, how it happened and why we missed it.

It is surely humanity's greatest achievement. If we could divert our eyes from our cellphones' news flashes more often, and look around us, at the science, technology and wealth that are now an integrated part of our lives, we would see proof of our abilities every day. So I borrow my dedication from the epitaph of Sir Christopher Wren, the architect who built and is buried in St Paul's Cathedral: *Si monumentum requiris, circumspice* ('If you are looking for a monument, look around you').

1
FOOD

[W]hoever could make two ears of corn, or two blades of grass, to grow upon a spot of ground, where only one grew before, would deserve better of mankind, and do more essential service to his country, than the whole race of politicians put together.

Jonathan Swift[1]

One winter's day in 1868 my great-great-great-great grandfather, Eric Norberg, returned to Nätra in northern Ångermanland, Sweden, with several bags of wheat flour in his cart. He came from a family of 'south carters', northern farmers who flouted Sweden's trade barriers and monopolies by going on long trading journeys. Eric Norberg sold country-woven linens in the south of Sweden and returned with salt and cereals.

Seldom, though, was his return so longed for as on this occasion. It was a famine year. Crops had failed everywhere in the country and those who were short of flour had to mix bark into their bread. A man from the neighbouring parish of Björna recalls his personal experience, aged seven, of those hungry years:

We often saw mother weeping to herself, and it was hard on a mother, not having any food to put on the table for her hungry children. Emaciated, starving children were often seen going from farm to farm, begging for a few crumbs of bread. One day three children came to us, crying and begging for something to still the pangs of hunger. Sadly, her eyes brimming with tears, our mother was forced to tell them that we had nothing but a few crumbs of bread which we ourselves needed. When we children saw the anguish in the unknown children's supplicatory eyes, we burst into tears and begged mother to share with them what crumbs we had. Hesitantly she acceded to our request, and the unknown children wolfed down the food before going on to the next farm, which was a good way off from our home. The following day all three were found dead between our farm and the next.[2]

Young and old, haggard and pale, went from farm to farm, begging for something to delay their death from starvation. The most emaciated livestock were tied upright because they could not stand on their own feet. Their milk was often mingled with blood. Several thousand Swedes died of starvation within that year and the next.

Failed harvests were not uncommon in Sweden. A single famine, between 1695 and 1697, claimed the lives of one in fifteen, and there are references to cannibalism in oral accounts. Without machinery, cold storage, irrigation or artificial fertilizers, crop failures were always a threat, and in the absence of modern communications and transportation, failed harvests often spelled famine.

Getting enough energy for the body and the brain to function well is the most basic human need, but historically, it has not been satisfied for most people. Famine was a universal, regular phenomenon, recurring so insistently in Europe that it

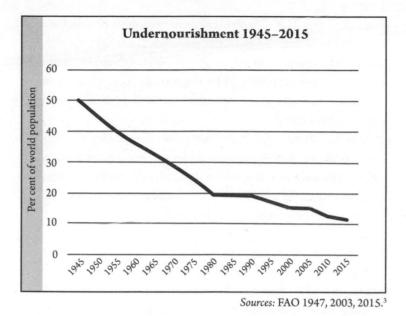

Sources: FAO 1947, 2003, 2015.[3]

'became incorporated into man's biological regime and built into his daily life', according to the French historian Fernand Braudel. France, one of the wealthiest countries in the world, suffered twenty-six national famines in the eleventh century, two in the twelfth, four in the fourteenth, seven in the fifteenth, thirteen in the sixteenth, eleven in the seventeenth and sixteen in the eighteenth. In each century, there were also hundreds of local famines.[4]

In times of famine, peasants from the countryside turned to the towns, where they crowded together and begged for food and often died in squares and streets, as in Venice and Amiens in the sixteenth century. The cold weather in the seventeenth century made the situation much worse. In 1694, a chronicler in Meulan, Normandy, noted that the hungry harvested the wheat before it was ripe, and 'large numbers of people lived on grass like animals'.[5] They might have been relatively lucky – in central France in 1662, 'Some people ate human flesh.'[6] In Finland, the years 1695–7 are known as 'the years of many deaths' when between a quarter and a third of the entire population died of famine.

Braudel points out that this was in privileged Europe; 'Things were far worse in Asia, China and India.' They were dependent on rice harvests crossing vast distances and every crisis became a disaster. Braudel quotes a Dutch merchant who witnessed the Indian famine of 1630–1:

'Men abandoned towns and villages and wandered helplessly. It was easy to recognize their condition: eyes sunk deep in the head, lips pale and covered with slime, the skin hard, with the bones showing through, the belly nothing but a pouch hanging down empty ... One would cry and howl for hunger, while another lay stretched on the ground dying in misery.' The familiar human dramas followed: wives and children abandoned, children sold by parents, who either abandoned them or sold themselves in order to survive, collective suicides ... Then came the stage when the starving split open the stomachs of the dead or dying and 'drew at the entrails to fill their own bellies'. 'Many hundred thousands of men died of hunger, so that the whole country was covered with corpses lying unburied, which caused such a stench that the whole air was filled and infected with it ... in the village of Susuntra ... human flesh was sold in open market.'[7]

Even in normal times margins in the most developed countries were exceedingly narrow, and the food not always very nutritious, nor could it be kept very long. Often it had to be procured just before eating. People dried and salted down their food for storage, but salt was expensive. In an ordinary home in my ancestors' province of Ångermanland a hundred years ago, there were four meals: potatoes, herring and bread for breakfast; porridge or gruel for lunch; potatoes, herring and bread for dinner; and porridge or gruel for supper. This is what people ate every day, except on Sundays, when they had meat soup (if there was any meat) mixed with barley grains. There being no china, everyone ate from the same dish, using a wooden spoon which was afterwards licked clean and put away in the table drawer.[8]

The importance of adequate nutrition for people's health and survival has been documented in a disturbing way by a study of life expectancy at the age of fifty in what are now rich countries, at the turn of the last century. It turns out that it is almost half a year longer for those born in the Northern Hemisphere between October and December than for those born between April and June. In the Southern Hemisphere, it is the other way around. Those born in the Northern Hemisphere, who later migrated to the South, also live longer if they were born between October and December. One of the probable reasons for this is that fresh fruit and vegetables were more readily available in the autumn until quite recently, even in rich countries. It seems that nutrition in the womb and early infancy was better for these children, since birth weights were also higher in the autumn.[9]

At the end of the eighteenth century, ordinary French families had to spend about half their income on grains alone – often this meant gruel. The French and English in the eighteenth century received fewer calories than the current average in sub-Saharan Africa, the region most tormented by undernourishment.[10]

If you sometimes hear about short working hours in the ancient past, don't be too envious. People worked as long as they could. The main limiting factor was that they did not have access to the calories they needed for children to grow properly or for adults to maintain healthy bodily functions. Our ancestors were stunted, skinny and short, which required fewer calories and made it possible to work with less food. The economist and Nobel laureate Angus Deaton, who is one of the world's leading experts on health and development, talks about a 'nutritional trap' in Britain in the eighteenth and early nineteenth century: because of this lack of calories people could not work hard enough to produce enough food to be able to work hard.[11]

It has been estimated that 200 years ago some twenty per cent of the inhabitants of England and France could not work at all. At most they had enough energy for a few hours of slow walking per day, which condemned most of them to a life of begging.[12] The lack of adequate nutrition had a serious effect on the population's intellectual development as well, since children's brains need fat to develop properly.

Some thinkers at the time assumed this would always be the case. In the eighteenth century, the Reverend Thomas Robert Malthus concluded that human numbers would always outrun the amount of food available. He saw that population doubled at an exponential rate – from two to four to eight to sixteen – whereas agricultural production only increased at a linear rate – from two to three to four to five. Whenever food was abundant it would result in more surviving children, which would result in even more deaths later on. Humanity would always suffer from famine, Malthus concluded in 1779:

The power of population is so superior to the power in the earth to produce subsistence for man, that premature death must in some shape or other visit the human race. The vices of humanity [infanticide, abortion, contraception] are active and able ministers of depopulation. They are the great precursors in the great army of destruction, and often finish the dreadful work themselves. But should they fail in this war of extermination, sickly seasons, epidemics, pestilence, and plague, advance in terrific array, and sweep off their thousands and ten thousands. Should success be still incomplete, gigantic inevitable famine stalks in the rear, and with one mighty blow, levels the population with the food of the world.[13]

Malthus accurately described humanity's predicament as it stood. But he underestimated its ability to innovate, solve problems and change its ways when Enlightenment ideas and expanded freedoms gave people the opportunity to do so. As farmers got individual property rights, they then had an incentive to produce more. As borders were opened to international trade, regions began to specialize in the kinds of production suited to their soil, climate and skills. And agricultural technology improved to make use of these opportunities. Even though population grew rapidly, the supply of food grew more quickly. The per capita consumption in France and English increased from around 1,700–2,200 calories in the mid-eighteenth century to 2,500–2,800 in 1850. Famines began to disappear.[14] Sweden was declared free from chronic hunger in the early twentieth century.[15]

However, as late as 1918, in a book about the food situation, the United States Food Administration published a 'Hunger Map of Europe', showing the threats to food security in Europe at the end of the First World War. A few countries, such as Britain, France, Spain and the Nordic countries, were deemed to have 'sufficient present food supply but future serious [shortages]'. Italy had a 'serious food shortage' and countries such as Finland, Poland and Czechoslovakia suffered from 'famine conditions'. 'Remember,' the book said, 'that every little country on the [map] is not merely an outline, but represents millions of people who are suffering from hunger.'[16]

One of the most powerful weapons against the scourge of hunger was artificial fertilizer. Nitrogen helps plants to grow and some of it is available in manure, but not much. For more than a century, the world's farmers used bird droppings accumulated over centuries on the coast of Chile, which contained huge quantities of sodium nitrate. But not enough of it was available. Scientists and entrepreneurs thought that there must be some way of fixing nitrogen from the atmosphere, where it is abundant.

The German chemist Fritz Haber, working at the chemical company BASF, was the first to solve the problem. Based on his theoretical work, and after several years of experiments, in 1909 he succeeded in producing ammonia from hydrogen and atmospheric nitrogen. The problem was that he could only do it on a very small scale. There were no large containers that functioned at the temperatures and pressures needed. A colleague at BASF, Carl Bosch, carried out over 20,000 experiments in over twenty reactors before he came up with the right process to synthesize ammonia on an industrial scale. The Haber-Bosch Process made artificial fertilizer cheap and abundant, and soon it was used all over the world.

'What has been the most important technical invention of the twentieth century?' asks Vaclav Smil in *Enriching the Earth*.

He rejects suggestions like computers and aeroplanes, going on to explain that nothing has been as important as the industrial fixing of nitrogen: 'the single most important change affecting the world's population – its expansion from 1.6 billion people in 1900 to today's six billion – would not have been possible without the synthesis of ammonia.' Without the Haber-Bosch Process about two-fifths of the world population would not exist at all, Smil claims.[17]

Sadly, Fritz Haber's brilliant mind was also put to the task of killing. He was a pioneer in chemical warfare and developed chlorine gas for the German troops to use against enemy forces. He directed the first release of fatal gas himself on 22 April 1915, at the Second Battle of Ypres. Six thousand French soldiers were killed. As Haber put it, 'During peace time a scientist belongs to the World, but during war time he belongs to his country.'[18] Coming from a man who saved more lives than perhaps anyone else, but also destroyed lives on a massive scale, this might be one of the best possible arguments against war.

There were downsides to artificial fertilizer as well. Nitrogen makes everything grow. Agricultural run-off from our coasts causes algae to bloom, which results in oxygen depletion as they decay. This has a serious effect on other organisms, and those that cannot escape from the environment become ecologically stressed or die out. From the northern Mexican Gulf to the Baltic Sea, we have seen more 'dead zones' like this in the last half century, which has resulted in tighter regulation of the use of nitrogen fertilizer in several countries.

But in parallel to this, every other form of agricultural technology has also improved. A hundred and fifty years ago it took twenty-five men all day to harvest and thresh a ton of grain.

With a modern combine harvester, a single person can do it in six minutes. In other words, it contributed to a 2,500-fold productivity increase. It used to take half an hour to milk ten litres. With modern milking machines it takes less than one minute.[19] Expanded trade, better infrastructure, cheap electricity and fuel, food packaging and refrigeration have all made it possible to move food from surplus areas to places with shortfalls. In the USA, it took about 1,700 hours to purchase the annual food supply for a family in the late nineteenth century. Today, it takes no more than 260 hours.[20]

In the mid-nineteenth century, the average daily calorific intake in western Europe was between 2,000 and 2,500 – below what it is in Africa today. In 1950, it was already around 3,000. One indicator of health is average height, since the human body reduces its growth if the necessary amount of nutrition is not available. The historical records show that the difference in height between western Europe and the rest of the world was marginal until about 1870. After that, the average western European grew in stature by around one centimetre per decade, from 167 centimetres to 179 centimetres a century later.[21] This was incredibly important for health, since taller people generally lived longer and children who received better nutrition could resist disease and stood a better chance of surviving.

It was not just an increase in food that saved us from Malthus's nightmares, but also lower fertility. As people became richer and better educated, they had *fewer* children, not more, as had been predicted. US fertility rates plummeted from seven children per woman in 1800 to 3.8 children in 1900, and to 1.9 children in 2012 – below the replacement rate. The trend is the same all over the Western world.[22] It seems that, when child health improved, parents could assume that their offspring would survive to adulthood, and as human capital increased in value, economically it made more sense to have fewer children and bestow them with a longer education instead. The argument of Malthus was turned on its head – food production exploded, but population growth slowed.

For the first time in humanity's history, the food problem was being solved. In some places it even started to be overtaken by the opposite problem – that of obesity. But still, many assumed that it would be impossible to feed the rest of the planet. As mortality rates plunged, a growing global population had to be fed. From 1950 to the mid-1980s, world population doubled from 2.5 to five billion, and many neo-Malthusians predicted mass starvation. 'The battle to feed all of humanity is over,' Paul Ehrlich wrote in *The Population Bomb* in 1968. 'In the 1970s, the world will undergo famines – hundreds of millions of people are going to starve to death.'[23] In *Famine 1975!* William and Paul Paddock predicted that 'in fifteen years the famines will be catastrophic'.[24]

Yet the exact opposite happened. Just when they said that the battle was lost, we made huge gains, and no one fought more bravely for humanity than Norman Borlaug, an agronomist from Iowa, who was obsessed with the problem of global hunger. In one episode of the TV series *Bullshit!* the magicians Penn and Teller play a game of 'The Greatest Person in History', with all the pretenders, religious leaders, presidents and revolutionary heroes in one deck. Like poker, each player places bets based on how good their cards are – but they might be bluffing. Penn draws one card and immediately goes all in, because he knows he is going to win. He got lucky: he drew Norman Borlaug.

The story of Borlaug and the global Green Revolution that he initiated begins in Mexico in 1944, when he started working there for the Rockefeller Foundation on agricultural development.[25] The programme was initiated to teach Mexican farmers new methods, but Borlaug was obsessed with coming up with better, higher-yield crops. He grew up in the US Midwest, and noticed that horrible dust storms and crop failures had the least impact where farmers had begun with high-yield approaches to farming. He wanted more countries to have access to this.

After thousands of crossings of wheat, Borlaug managed to come up with a high-yield hybrid that was parasite resistant and wasn't sensitive to daylight hours, so it could be grown in varying climates. Importantly, it was a dwarf variety, since tall wheat expended a lot of energy growing inedible stalks and also collapsed when it grew too quickly. When he introduced this new hybrid, Borlaug also showed farmers how modern irrigation and artificial fertilizer increased the yields. The new wheat was quickly introduced all over Mexico, and amazingly in 1963, the harvest was six times larger than in 1944. Overnight, Mexico became a net exporter of wheat.

Borlaug worked in the developing world for most of his life, spreading these technologies, but he struggled against local mores, feudal traditions, hostility to Westerners, and often Westerners themselves, who claimed that a better food supply would cause overpopulation, and it would be better to let nature do its work.

In 1963, Borlaug moved on to India and Pakistan, just as it found itself facing the threat of massive starvation. Immediately, he ordered thirty-five trucks of high-yield seeds to be driven from Mexico to Los Angeles, in order to ship them from there. First, the convoy was held up by Mexican police and then blocked at the US border because of a ban on seed imports. Then it was stopped by the National Guard, because riots had blocked the harbour. But in the end, the ship sailed. That was only the beginning of the problems, however: 'I went to bed thinking the problem was at last solved,' Borlaug said, 'and woke up to the news that war had broken out between India and Pakistan.'

But Borlaug and his team worked tirelessly throughout the war, planting seeds sometimes within sight of artillery flashes. Despite a late planting and the many logistical problems, yields rose by seventy per cent that year, enough to prevent a general wartime famine. Because of the risk of wartime starvation, he got the go-ahead from both governments to roll it out on a larger scale. The next harvest was even bigger, and the food situation was beginning to come under control. Suddenly there was a shortage of labour to harvest all the crops, and a dearth of everything from jute bags to railcars. Some school buildings had to be closed temporarily, so they could be used for grain storage.

Just a few years later the impossible had happened, and India and Pakistan were self-sufficient in the production of cereals. Today they produce seven times more wheat than they did in 1965. Despite a rapidly growing population, both countries are much better fed than they used to be.

Borlaug also convinced many governments to pay their farmers world market prices for their grain, rather than forcing them to sell at a fixed, low price. This widespread price regulation was a policy intended to help the urban population, but resulted in lower production and hunger. Inspired by his success with better crops, colleagues of Borlaug developed high-yield rice varieties that quickly spread around Asia.

This was the Green Revolution, which has given poor countries better crops and bigger yields, and has alleviated rural poverty. The average global daily intake of calories was 2,200 in

1961, but has since increased to more than 2,800. Back then, people in fifty-one countries, including Iran, Pakistan, China and Indonesia, consumed less than 2,000 calories per person, per day. By 2013, that number had fallen to just one: Zambia. Even after the increase in food prices in the last few years, world agricultural prices (as measured by the Grilli-Yang Index) are now half of what they were in the early twentieth century.[26]

The Food and Agricultural Organization of the United Nations (FAO) reported in 1947 that around fifty per cent of the world's population was chronically malnourished.[27] Around this time, nitrogen fertilizer was introduced broadly and many low- and middle-income countries began to modernize their agricultural sectors. In 1969–71, the FAO estimated that thirty-seven per cent of the developing world population was undernourished, and today this has declined to around thirteen per cent.

Table 1. Undernourishment, percentage of population

	1969–71	1979–81	1990–2	2000–2	2014–16
Latin America	20	14	15	11	6
Asia	40	30	24	18	12
Africa	34	31	28	25	20
Developing world	37	28	23	18	13
World	29	19	19	15	11

Sources: FAO 2003, 2015.

Since 1990–2, the proportion of chronically undernourished people has declined from twenty-three to thirteen per cent of the global low- and middle-income country population. The number of hungry people has been reduced by 216 million. Since the population has grown by 1.9 billion people at the same time, the FAO estimates that about two billion people have been freed from a likely state of hunger in the past twenty-five years.

One country that has seen more progress than others is Peru, which has reduced malnutrition by seventy-six per cent since 1990. Today, 4.7 million fewer Peruvians experience under-nourishment. One reason is that Peru introduced an open trade regime, property rights and transactions reform, which gave more farmers access to credit and incentives to improve their farms. As a result, agricultural productivity has soared. Similar reforms in Vietnam, including the opening up of the rice market and reduced agricultural taxes, have reduced the number suffering from malnutrition there by more than twenty million people.

Africa has the worst indicators. Hunger in Africa south of the Sahara decreased from thirty-three to twenty-three per cent from 1990 to 2014, but because of the increase in population, the number of chronically undernourished people has increased by almost forty-five million. However, there are success stories in Africa too. Even though the population grew by more than eighty million in Nigeria between 1990 and 2015, the number of undernourished people declined by around eight million. Countries such as Angola, Cameroon and Mozambique cut their rate of malnutrition by more than fifty per cent.

After the Second World War, average height started to increase in developing countries, just as it had in rich countries before them. In East Asia it increased from 166 centimetres in the 1930s to 172 in the 1980s. In Japan it increased by ten centimetres in just fifty years. In sub-Saharan Africa, by contrast, average height actually decreased by one centimetre between the 1960s and the 1980s. Interestingly, there is a clear correlation between height and GDP per capita (though it plateaus in wealthy countries).[28] The prevalence of child stunting – when malnutrition stops children's growth – has declined by twenty-five per cent since 2000.[29]

It has been estimated that in the first decade of the twentieth century, 3.1 million children died annually because of conditions related to malnutrition. This increased to about four million children in the 1950s and 1960s because of population growth, but then it started to decline rapidly, even in absolute numbers. In the first decade of the twenty-first century, 1.7 million children died because of malnutrition – still a shockingly high number, but a sixty per cent reduction since the 1950s, even though world population more than doubled.[30]

There have been negative side effects of this more intensive farming, including over-extraction of groundwater for irrigation and nitrate pollution of water bodies. But the Green Revolution also made it possible to save pristine land from being turned into farmland. Between 1700 and 1960, farmland quadrupled, as people made use of forests and grassland to feed themselves. But after fixing nitrogen and developing new seeds, it was possible to produce more from the same amount of land. For the first time, for the world as a whole, food production has been decoupled from land use.

From 1961 to 2009, farmland increased by only twelve per cent, while farm production increased by about 300%. It has been estimated that, had agricultural yields stayed the same, farmers would have needed to turn another three billion hectares into farmland – immense continental areas, about the size of the USA, Canada and China put together. Artificial fertilizer has caused oxygen depletion in many marine systems, but it also saved us from depleting wildlife and turning our planet into 'Skinhead Earth'.[31]

In 1970, Borlaug won the Nobel Peace Prize for his work in increasing the global food supply. As US Senator Rudy Boschwitz put it:

> Dr. Norman Borlaug is the first person in history to save a billion human lives. But he must also get credit for saving the wild creatures and diverse plant species on 12 million square miles of global forest that would long since have been ploughed down without the high-yield farming he pioneered. The two accomplishments combined make him dramatically unique.[32]

Nonetheless, arguments against modern agricultural technology have had a huge impact on the debate, and some environmentalists object to nitrogen fertilizer on principle, despite the human cost. Today we see the same objections to genetically modified crops, which would increase our yields even further. Environmental campaigners have had an impact on one continent, Africa, where they pressured big foundations and the World Bank to back away from introducing the Green Revolution, which Borlaug had considered the next priority. This is now the only region where the number of undernourished people has continued to increase, and where wild habitats are being depleted by slash-and-burn subsistence agriculture.

Borlaug has reacted angrily to this campaign:

> Some of the environmental lobbyists of the Western nations are the salt of the earth, but many of them are elitists. They've never experienced the physical sensation of hunger. They do

their lobbying from comfortable office suites in Washington or Brussels. If they lived just one month amid the misery of the developing world, as I have for fifty years, they'd be crying out for tractors and fertilizer and irrigation canals and be outraged that fashionable elitists back home were trying to deny them these things.[33]

Borlaug has succeeded in privately funding several African projects since the early 1990s, with the help of former US president Jimmy Carter and the Japanese philanthropist Ryoichi Sasakawa. At first Borlaug thought they should start with a few years of research, but after he saw the terrible circumstances there, he changed his mind and proposed that they 'just start growing' and proceeded to triple corn yields. One of his most successful projects has focused on Ethiopia. It is now one of a few African countries that have managed to reach the Millennium Development Goal of halving the proportion in hunger between 1990 and 2015. Almost six million fewer Ethiopians face chronic hunger today than in 1990, even though the population has increased by more than forty million.

Quite possibly, the most important long-term effect of the Green Revolution was that it reduced the number of mouths that had to be fed, long-term. When children began to survive to adulthood, parents began to have fewer children. The demographic transition that the West has already gone through is now being repeated across the developing world. The neo-Malthusians claimed this wouldn't happen at all, but in fact it has happened much *faster* in low- and middle-income countries.

Between 1950–5 and 2010–15, the number of children per woman declined from 6.1 to 2.6. The unprecedented demographic transition that took the Western world 200 years was repeated by the developing world in just sixty years. In East Asia, it declined from 5.6 to 1.6, in South Asia from 6 to 2.6, and in Latin America from 5.9 to 2.2. The region where the transition has been slower is also the one with the least progress in wealth, health and education, but even in sub-Saharan Africa the fertility rate has declined, from 6.6 to 5.1, and according to the UN projections, it will decline to four in 2030 and to three in 2050.[34] The combination of more food per hectare and smaller families will mean that the increase in farmland has almost slowed to a halt, which will be a huge boon to biological diversity in the coming century.

Even better news than the decline of chronic undernourishment is the disappearance of major famines. Over the last 140 years, there were 106 episodes of mass starvation that each killed more than 100,000 people. From 1900 to 1909, twenty-seven million people died in famines, and more than fifteen million died every decade from the 1920s to the 1960s. Those famines were often partly or wholly man-made.[35] In the earliest era this was a result of imperial policies that dismantled local farm production and trade and forced peasants to produce for exports. War famines killed millions in Asia in the 1930s and 1940s. Communist regimes in the Soviet Union, China, Cambodia, Ethiopia and North Korea killed tens of millions because of forced collectivization and the use of hunger as a weapon.

In our own time, the most ruthless regimes still produce the most horrific conditions. Jang Jin-sung, a member of North Korea's élite, described what he saw in the late 1990s, before he fled to the West. The starving were sent to parks to beg until they died. A special 'Corpse Division' would poke at bodies with sticks to see if they were already dead. He saw them loading corpses on a rickshaw, on which bare and skeletal feet poked out in odd directions.

In a crowded market, Jang saw an adult woman and a girl of about seven. The woman had hung a sign around the girl's neck: 'I will sell my daughter for 100 won' – less than ten pence. Apparently, the father had already died of starvation. An army lieutenant agreed to take the girl. The mother ran away with the money, but soon returned with a packet of bread. She asked her daughter for forgiveness, sobbing violently while she began to put pieces of bread into the child's mouth: 'This is all I can give you before I go.' Several in the crowd began to cry.[36]

But the experience of North Korea is an outlier: in general, communism has collapsed and empires have fallen. Farmers have received the formal titles to their land, which has given them an incentive to invest in better equipment and irrigation systems. Trade across borders and within countries has made it possible for other regions to supply those that have a temporary shortage, so that today, those in the position of my ancestor needn't travel hundreds of miles in search of food.

The death toll from great famines declined to 1.4 million during the 1990s. In the twenty-first century, thus far, the death toll is near 600,000 – just two per cent of what it was 100 years earlier, even though world population is four times bigger than it was then. These modern famines are the result of armed conflicts in countries such as Sudan, Somalia and the Democratic Republic of Congo.[37]

Strange as it sounds, democracy is one of our most potent weapons against famine. As the economist Amartya Sen has pointed out, there have been famines in communist states, absolute monarchies, colonial states and tribal societies, but never in a democracy. Even poor democracies, such as India and Botswana, have avoided starvation despite having a poorer food supply than many countries where disaster has struck. Rulers who are dependent on voters do everything to avoid starvation, and a free press makes the public aware of the problems, so that they can be tackled in time. In authoritarian states, by contrast, there have sometimes been famines for the simple reason that the rulers have believed their own propaganda, and no one dares to tell them that people are starving.[38]

There is probably no country that has suffered greater famine than China. From 1958 to 1961, the dictator Mao Zedong tried to show the superiority of his brand of communism by a 'Great Leap Forward' of forced industrialization. Remaining private land and even cooking utensils were confiscated and agricultural workers were diverted to steel making and public works projects. As a result, around forty million people are estimated to have starved to death, and life expectancy collapsed by twenty years.

Even after this disaster, food was scarce in China because the collective farms stifled work and innovation. No one could make more by working harder or investing in better methods. Today, China's leaders are proud of its productive agricultural sector, but it did not change because of a top-down decision. It was started by a few brave peasants in the Xiaogang village in Anhui province in December 1978.

The eighteen families of the village were desperate. The communist system did not supply them or their children with enough to eat. Some families had to boil poplar leaves and eat them with salt; others ground roasted tree bark to use as flour. So they met in secret late one night and agreed to parcel out the communal land among themselves. Every family would make its own decisions on what and how to farm and how much to work, and each family would be allowed to sell what they produced themselves, after the government took the share it demanded.

They wrote it down as a formal contract so that everyone would be bound to it, and signed or gave their fingerprints by the light of an oil lamp. Now that it was down in writing, the stakes were incredibly high. If the document was found, they would be punished with the full weight of the regime. The villagers agreed that if word got out and any of them were jailed or executed, the others would raise their children. The farmer who had drawn up the contract hid it inside a piece of bamboo in the roof of his house, and hoped that the officials would never find it.

In the end, word of this secret privatization got out. The result was just too good to keep a secret. The farmers did not start the workday when the village whistle blew any longer – they went out much earlier and worked much harder. There was a dramatic surge in production. Grain output in 1979 was six times higher than the year before. Other villages could see that Xiaogang did better, and that people there were better fed, and tried to find out what they had done differently. Individual farming spread 'like a chicken pest', as one farmer put it. 'When one village has it, the whole country will be infected.'[39]

The communist party was hostile to individual initiative and should have punished the farmers. But the grassroots reforms were incredibly popular and the party realized this was the only way to put an end to hunger and inefficiency. In 1982, in an unprecedented about-turn, the party endorsed the reforms, and allowed other villages to do the same. Two years later, there were no communes left in China. A country that experienced one of the worst famines in history just two decades earlier now produced a surplus of food for the world markets.

Guan Youjiang, one of the original signatories of the Xiaogang agreement, remembers that people used to die of hunger in his village. He used to roam the countryside begging. The freedom to choose one's work, and to reap the rewards, made all the difference. 'Before, farmers were happy if they had a meal a day. Now they have three – and sometimes a drink too.'[40]

2

SANITATION

It is things going right that is poetical! Our digestions, for instance, going sacredly and silently right, that is the foundation of all poetry. Yes, the most poetical thing, more poetical than the flowers, more poetical than the stars – the most poetical thing in the world is not being sick.

G. K. Chesterton[1]

Food is not enough to sustain life. You also need a safe way of dealing with refuse and waste, without which life is just as miserable, and potentially just as short.

Water is the source of all life, but throughout history it has also been a source of great suffering, since even in small settlements it becomes contaminated by human waste and spreads bacteria, viruses, parasites and worms. The lack of access to safe drinking water is one reason for the historic popularity of beer and wine before coffee made its entrance in the seventeenth century. At least alcohol didn't kill you.

As far back as the Ancient Greeks, people realized that wounds treated with wine were less likely to become infected than those treated with water. Typhoid was spread by eating food or drinking water contaminated with the faeces of an infected person, and this illness alone killed about a quarter of all patients. It may have been the disease that killed every third Athenian in 430 BCE and ended its golden period. More recently, typhoid killed Queen Victoria's husband, Prince Albert, at the age of forty-two. Cholera spread from the Indian subcontinent and water contaminated with the bacterium has killed tens of millions since the early nineteenth century.

Safe water is essential not just for drinking, but also for daily personal and domestic hygiene and food preparation. Most of the illness in the world is still caused by waterborne diseases, and the World Health Organization (WHO) estimates that at any given time almost half the population in low- and middle-income countries are suffering from diseases related to inadequate provision of safe water and sanitation services. In fact, diarrhoea is a leading cause of mortality among children under five years old.

A textbook on health states: 'Though difficult to quantify, it seems that the main environmental health problem in the world is still unsafe, microbial contaminated water for drinking and household use, combined with a lack of adequate sanitation for the disposal of waste, faeces, and urine.'[2]

In the medieval English village, homes had no privy, so people would walk 'a bowshot from the house' when they had to go. Some people used chamber pots, and in some places there were open trenches with simple seats. In the homes of the rich and powerful, the latrines were often situated under the dining room, which gave a whiff of danger to every dinner party. In 1183, for instance, the Holy Roman Emperor Frederick II organized a great feast while holding court in a castle in Erfurt, Germany. While the guests were eating, the floor of the great hall began to sink and many noble guests fell into the cesspit beneath. Many drowned in the slurry.

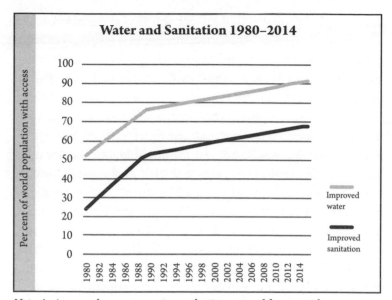

Note: An improved water source is one that is protected from outside contamination; improved sanitation is a system that separates excreta from human contact.

Sources: WHO 1995, 2015.[3]

Flush toilets have been used in many civilizations, including the Roman Empire, but the modern water closet was invented in 1596 for Queen Elizabeth I by her godson Sir John Harrington. In the absence of an extensive sewer system it wasn't very useful. Indoor plumbing and widespread installation of water closets would take another 300 years. There are contemporaneous accounts of aristocrats soiling the corridors of Versailles and the Palais Royal. Indeed, the reason why Versailles's hedges were so tall was so that they could function as toilet partitions. One eighteenth-century writer described Versailles as 'the receptacle of all of humanity's horrors – the passageways, corridors and courtyards are filled with urine and faecal matter.'[4]

Until modern times, taking a bath was rare, even controversial. The Spanish saw it as a Muslim custom, and the French thought that it softened the body and opened the pores to disease. It was seen as more hygienic for the élite to change clothes often and wear them tight. But there were some early adopters. Queen Elizabeth I is said to have taken a bath once a month whether she thought she needed it or not, and one member of the British élite wrote in his diary in 1653 that he would start experimenting with an 'annual hair wash'.[5] As late as 1882, only two per cent of New York's homes had water connections.[6]

Water wells were often dug close to the farmhouse, which meant that they were also close to the barnyard, stable, pigsty and cesspool, so all sorts of matter seeped through the ground. But it was the concentration of people in cities that made sanitary problems acute. Writers at the time described Europe's greatest cities as filled with huge piles of human and animal excrement, their rivers and lakes as foetid swamps, often solid with waste. Several travellers from the countryside recorded that their first intimation of important cities was the stink. Waste would be dumped into city streets and rain would wash it into the local watershed. In 1900 horses supposedly fouled New York City streets with more than 2.5 million pounds of manure and 60,000 gallons of urine daily. The streets were carpeted with the stuff.[7]

Toilets were built by rivers and brooks, which polluted the waterways, and if a river was not available, the filth was held in cesspits or thrown out on the street. When pedestrians heard the shout of 'Gardyloo!' they ran for cover. This phrase, taken from the French for 'Look out for the water', was your only warning that someone was about to throw their waste out of the window.

The area surrounding the Royal Dramatic Theatre and Nybroviken is one of the loveliest and most prosperous in all of Stockholm. On a bright summer's day you can stroll along the quayside and watch the sun glittering in the deep blue water round the boats preparing to take tourists on tours of the archipelago. It is hard to imagine that Nybroviken 200 years ago was one of the sewers of the city. Ships' captains complained from time to time over the difficulty of steering ships in water so clogged up with filth and debris. One day in 1827 a passing doctor was appalled to see women washing their laundry in the dirty brown water: 'I say nothing of how pure and healthy the linen can be from daily washing in Nybroviken, the water of which, from the dissolution of its faecal admixture, has the viscosity of red lead, but it is horrifying to see that the water there is being fetched even for cooking.'[8]

The early sanitarian movement had no science on which to base its work, so it relied on the theory of 'miasma' – that if it smelled bad it was bad for health. Although the underlying theory was false, it did contain a grain of truth. It was important that human waste was disposed of safely, and efforts to make sure that water did not stink probably did much to make it safer as well. But unfortunately it also made things worse in some instances. London's early sewage systems ended the practice of keeping cesspools in basements, but they did so by dumping raw sewage into the River Thames, also the source of the city's drinking water. In this way, cholera was recycled into the water supply. Two outbreaks of cholera in London between 1848 and 1854 killed 25,000 people.

This tragedy made one of the world's great medical experiments possible, 'one of the most important of all time', according to Angus Deaton.[9] John Snow, a physician in London, thought that cholera was borne by water rather than foul air. He mapped the deaths in detail and found a revealing link. All the cholera cases seemed to originate from the water company that had its inlet downstream of the sewage discharge, whereas no deaths were found among those who got their water from the other company, which had recently moved its inlet to purer water upriver. This convinced the local council to disable the offending well pump. The discovery of waterborne infection has since saved countless lives.

The major push for a modern sewerage system came after 'The Great Stink' in the summer of 1858, when the hot weather exacerbated the smell from the Thames and created a stench so bad that the curtains of the Houses of Parliament had to be soaked in lime chloride. The Chancellor of the Exchequer, Benjamin Disraeli, compared the Thames to the river running through hell in Greek mythology: 'a Stygian pool, reeking with ineffable and intolerable horrors'.[10]

During the late nineteenth and early twentieth century, many cities built modern water and sewer systems and began systematic garbage collection. Rising wealth made such costly ventures possible. The major change, though, came with the effective filtering and chlorination of water supplies in the first half of the twentieth century, after the germ theory of disease had been accepted. Life expectancy increased more rapidly in the USA during this period than in any other period in American history, and the introduction of filters and chlorination shows that clean water played a decisive role. One study found that clean water was responsible for forty-three per cent of the total reduction in mortality, seventy-four per cent of the infant mortality reduction and sixty-two per cent of the child mortality reduction.[11]

This technological shift came late to low- and middle-income countries, but once begun, it happened faster than it once had in the wealthiest countries. The proportion of the world population with access to an improved water source has increased from fifty-two to ninety-one per cent between 1980 and 2015. Since 1990, 2.6 billion people have gained access to an improved water source, which means that 285,000 more people got safe water *every day* for twenty-five years. Depending on how fast you read, another 300 to 900 people will have got access to safe water for the first time before you have reached the end of this chapter.

In fact, forty-one per cent of the current population in low- and middle-income countries have gained coverage in the last thirty years. There are now only three countries (that give accurate data) with less than fifty per cent coverage: Namibia, Equatorial Guinea and Papua New Guinea – compared with twenty-three in 1990. Today, ninety-six per cent of the urban population have access, and eighty-four per cent of the rural population.[12]

In 1980, no more than twenty-four per cent of the world's population had access to proper sanitation facilities. By 2015, this had increased to sixty-eight per cent. Nearly a third of the current global population gained access in the last twenty-five years – 2.1 billion people. Eighty-two per cent of the urban population now have access, compared to fifty-one per cent of the rural population. A quarter of those in rural areas still practice open defecation, though this has been reduced from thirty-eight per cent in 1990. Countries such as India, Pakistan, Bangladesh and Vietnam have reduced open defecation by around a third since 1990.

As a result of these efforts, global deaths from diarrhoea have been reduced from 1.5 million in 1990 to 622,000 in 2012. But pre-modern conditions still afflict hundreds of millions of people around the world – 663 million people still lack access to improved water sources, and depend on unprotected wells, springs and surface water. Unimproved sanitation facilities are still used by 2.4 billion people.

In the modern era, water shortages are rarely about water, and more often due to bad policies and the lack of proper technology. In a book on water pricing, Fredrik Segerfeldt points out that countries such as Cambodia, Rwanda and Haiti have problems in giving people access to safe water even though they have much more rainfall than Australia, where everybody has access. Cherrapunji in India is the wettest place on earth, yet it has repeated water shortages.[13]

More than eighty per cent of the freshwater in developing countries is used for agriculture, and only around one per cent of irrigation agriculture uses the most efficient drip irrigation system, so most of that water is wasted. One major problem is that underpricing – and sometimes zero pricing – reduces the incentive to invest in water-saving technologies and results in overuse. As the United Nations Development Programme points out: 'if markets delivered Porsche cars at give-away prices, they too would be in short supply'.[14]

Better water access is not just about health. It is also about opportunities in life, especially for women, who in many areas are responsible for the heavy burden of providing the household with water. It has been estimated that collectively African women and children spend forty billion hours per year fetching and carrying water. This time is taken from work, leisure and child care. A common reason why young girls do not go to school is that their families demand that they fetch water from far-away sources. Another important reason given is that schools do not have suitable hygiene facilities.[15]

The greatest proportion without water and sanitation lives in sub-Saharan Africa. When I walk around Kibera, in Nairobi, Kenya, one of Africa's largest urban slums, I meet people who have to take an hour or more per day just to locate a water vendor and wait in line to be served. Some pay as much as a tenth or even a fifth of their income to get water. The inhabitants of Kibera were never granted deeds to land, so the buildings are outside the law, with little access to infrastructure and without the security in their possessions that would make investments in these areas possible.

Everywhere in Kibera I notice open sewers. When it is raining, the waste flows through the streets. Instead of toilets, there are latrines, not much more than holes in the ground with planks across for people to put their feet on. They can be shared by several hundred people, and they are often full of waste and reeking with urine. When they are full, they are emptied into the river. Women are afraid to go, especially at night, and children fear falling inside, which sadly they often do.

For all these reasons, Kibera has its own version of 'Gardyloo!', called 'flying toilets'. Kiberans relieve themselves in black polythene bags and at night they throw them away as far from their home as possible. The neighbour in turn sometimes throws it further away, and so on, until it is out of sight. The rain often washes them down into the river. When you walk around in the mornings you see piles of flying toilets in alleyways and on rooftops, from which people also harvest rainwater. Children play with these wrapped bags as balls during leisure time.

The flying toilet contributes to disease and early death in Kibera and many other slums around the world. The most common diseases in Kibera are all environment-related. Infant mortality is three times higher than in the rest of Nairobi. But even a local health worker admits to using the flying toilet all the time: 'At night, it is so dark in Kibera that you cannot dare to get out of your room since you are not sure if you will fall in one of the abandoned toilets and, as a woman, you can never be sure that you will not be raped.'[16]

But things are changing even here. Two water pipes have been constructed, so Kiberans do not have to rely entirely on the unsafe water from the dam and from the rain. Several modern sanitation blocs have been built by entrepreneurs and non-governmental organizations (NGOs), where Kiberans can go to a clean toilet and get a hot shower at a low cost, and hand-washing facilities have been introduced in several schools. Cases of typhoid, dysentery and hookworm infestations are on the decline, and at last, so is child and infant mortality.

Sub-Saharan Africa achieved a twenty-percentage-point increase in the use of improved sources of drinking water from 1990 to 2015. During this period, 427 million more Africans gained access.[17] The process may be too slow to make the news, but we must remember that it is happening much faster than it did in the world's richest countries. Life expectancy in Kenya increased by almost ten years between 2003 and 2013. After having lived, loved and struggled for a whole decade, the average person in Kenya had not lost a single year of their remaining lifetime. Everyone got ten years older, yet death had not come a step closer.

3

LIFE EXPECTANCY

> So in the face of overwhelming odds, I'm left with only one
> option: I'm going to have to science the shit out of this.
>
> Matt Damon in *The Martian*

Throughout humanity's early history, life was nasty, brutish
and short. More than anything, it was short, because of disease,
lack of food and lack of sanitation.

People died early, as infants or children, and mothers often
died giving birth. The high mortality rate was not primarily
because of the prevalence of violence, but because of infectious
disease, unsafe water and bad sanitary conditions. People lived
close to animals, even in cities, and their waste infected their
water sources.

Many lived in damp houses and slept on the ground in
timbered cottages. It may look romantic, but built of unsea-
soned wood, with tiny windows and almost no ventilation,
they were a mass of dirt and infested with all kinds of vermin.
As one historian put it: 'From a health point of view the only
thing to be said in their favour was that they burnt down easily.'[1]

All large towns regularly suffered from the plague, an infectious disease caused by bacteria that spread in the air and by

physical contact, and was carried by the fleas on rats. The disease killed three out of five of its victims. The worst instance was of course the Black Death in the mid-fourteenth century, which probably killed more than a third of Europe's population, and emptied entire villages and regions. One eyewitness in London reported that healthy people suddenly collapsed and that: 'between Candlemas [2 February 1349] and Easter [12 April], more than 200 corpses were buried almost every day in the new burial ground made next to Smithfield, and this was in addition to the bodies buried in other churchyards in the city.'[2]

To some, it literally seemed like the end of the world. In 1349, an Irish monk, surrounded by death, recorded the events and left his text with the words: 'I leave parchment for continuing the work, in case anyone should still be alive in the future and any son of Adam can escape this pestilence and continue the work.' After the text, there is a note in the copyist's handwriting saying: 'Here it seems the author died.'[3]

Even though this was the most devastating occurrence, plague would come back to haunt towns again and again until the eighteenth century. In Besançon, in eastern France, plague was reported forty times between 1439 and 1640. The moment people heard about an outbreak they fled, leaving the poor and the weak behind. Magistrates, lawyers, officers and other authority figures left their castles unprotected and their towns to fight for themselves. Chateaux were looted and doomed houses were marked, sometimes with a cross in red chalk. The dead were thrown on carts, loaded onto boats, put to sea and burned. In extreme situations bodies were just left in the streets, rotting and gnawed by dogs.

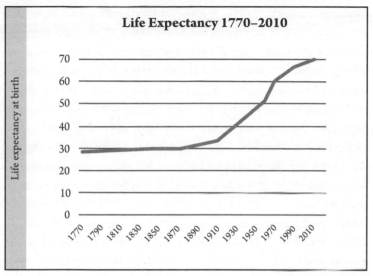

Source: Roser 2016.[4]

In 1586, the essayist Montaigne had to leave Bordeaux, where he was mayor, when the plague arrived. He and his family wandered around for six months in search of somewhere to live, but merely frightened old friends and caused horror wherever they appeared. In Savoy, rich people would first install a poor woman in their disinfected house for a few weeks, as a guinea pig, before they returned. Samuel Pepys wrote about 'the plague making us cruel, as dogs, one to another'.[5]

Tuberculosis, an infectious disease affecting the lungs, spread throughout Europe in the seventeenth century and was a major killer in the nineteenth century. Some estimates say it caused nearly a quarter of all deaths. Smallpox, another major cause of death, was a permanent presence in large cities. In smaller towns and villages it was not, but that meant no one developed immunity, so whole communities could be wiped out when they faced an epidemic.

Before evidence-based medicine, prayer was the commonest medicine. The wealthy could afford the best physicians, but for 2,000 years, these had little to offer beyond their bedside manner and bloodletting, as a surplus of blood was thought to cause fevers, headache, apoplexy and other illnesses. The physician tied the patient's arm to make the veins swell and then cut him and drained him of a certain amount of blood, which of course was often harmful. Sometimes leeches were used to extract the blood. In France, doctors used thirty million leeches in 1846 alone. There was no anaesthetic to make a surgical operation bearable, and when surgery became more common in the mid-nineteenth century many died from infection since there were no antibiotics (and in any case, the medical community still believed disease was spread by 'miasma'). The head, chest and stomach could not be operated on reliably. Injured limbs were amputated. There were no targeted drugs or transplants. Ageing meant losing one's mobility and eyesight.

In prehistoric times, the average hunter-gatherer is estimated to have had a life expectancy of around twenty to thirty years depending on local conditions.[6] Despite an often more stable supply of food, the agricultural revolution did not improve this much, and according to some accounts reduced it, since larger, settled groups were more exposed to infectious disease and problems related to sanitation. In classical civilizations such as Ancient Greece and the Roman Empire, life expectancy has been estimated at around eighteen to twenty-five years. In medieval Britain, estimates range from seventeen to thirty-five years.[7]

The early era of globalization resulted in terrible epidemics, since populations which had earlier been separated now exchanged contagious germs. Europeans introduced smallpox to the Americas, and got syphilis in return. Plague came with the Mongol conquests and cholera spread on merchant routes from India, killing tens of millions from the early nineteenth century. Before the late nineteenth century, even those in the most advanced nations did not experience mortality much lower than was typical during most of our species' history. In the 1830s, life expectancy in western Europe was thirty-three years and it improved only slowly. Before the year 1800, not a single country in the world had a life expectancy higher than forty years.

But then, something amazing happened. A research group on ageing led by Oskar Burger at the Max Planck Institute has pointed out that the bulk of humanity's mortality reduction has been experienced by only the last four of the roughly 8,000 generations of homo sapiens since we evolved around 200,000 years ago. Since then, progress in extending human lifespans has been on par with or even exceeded what has been achieved by other species in laboratories when they have been exposed by scientists to dietary and selection experiments specially designed to extend lifespans.[8]

For most of history, parents often had to bury their children. Even though people must have hardened their attitude to death when they were constantly surrounded by it, the loss of one's children is a terrible blow in any era. The horrified reaction of Charles Darwin, who lost three of his ten children, to the death of his eldest daughter Annie, shows what a tragedy it can be for any parent, no matter how common, no matter how large the family. In Sweden in the early nineteenth century between thirty and forty per cent of all children died before their fifth birthday. In the early twentieth century, fifteen per cent did. Today, 0.3% do.[9]

Average life expectancy in the world was thirty-one years in 1900. Today, amazingly, it is seventy-one years. We instinctively assume that we approach death by one year for every year we age, but during the twentieth century, the average person approached death by just seven months for every year they aged. The years we gain are also qualitatively better. Chronic diseases among Americans today are not just less severe than they were a hundred years ago, but they also begin an average of ten years later in life.[10]

A professor of epidemiology, Abdel Omran, has divided humanity's relationship with mortality into three major successive stages:[11]

1. *The Age of Pestilence and Famine.* In this era, which was in place for most of humanity's history, mortality is high and fluctuating, as a result of chronic malnutrition and endemic diseases and sudden disasters like famines and war. Life expectancy is vacillating between twenty and forty years.

2. *The Age of Receding Pandemics.* Now mortality begins to decline as epidemics recede. Life expectancy increases steadily from about thirty to about fifty years. As a result, population growth is sustained.

3. *The Age of Degenerative and Man-Made Diseases.* Infectious disease becomes rarer, mortality declines further and life expectancy exceeds fifty years. Fertility, not mortality, becomes the crucial factor in population growth. We begin to worry about cancer and an increasing number of cardiovascular diseases, which is actually great news, because that

is a sign that people aren't expecting to die at the age of twenty or thirty.

The richest parts of the world, which were the most open to new knowledge wherever it came from, north-western Europe and its offshoots, went through these transitions first, from the eighteenth century and onwards. One reason was sanitary improvements. Wooden houses were replaced by brick and stone buildings, and villages began to hold water supplies separate from their waste and animals separate from homes. New standards for cleanliness were developed and people began to take baths. In the early eighteenth century the plague disappeared from western Europe.

But the health revolution was also a result of new medical knowledge and technology. Enlightenment thinkers encouraged the experimental method and evidence-based science, which proved that bloodletting was not beneficial and showed more effective ways of dealing with illness.

The battle against smallpox is one example. Smallpox was a widespread cause of death in Europe in the eighteenth century – some 400,000 people died annually and one-third of the survivors went blind. The great majority of all infants who got smallpox died. In Constantinople (now Istanbul), Lady Mary Wortley Montagu, the wife of Britain's ambassador, had seen variolation against smallpox at work and she studied it carefully since smallpox had killed her brother and scarred her own face. She inoculated her children and pressed for its introduction back home.

The procedure meant that material was extracted from the pustules of a bearer of smallpox and scratched into the arm of the patient, who got a mild case of smallpox and thereafter developed immunity. Around two per cent of those variolated died, but since almost a third of those suffering from smallpox usually died, this presented tremendous progress. After the British royal family was variolated in 1721, the practice spread rapidly and soon ordinary people were also inoculated.[12]

An eight-year-old boy was variolated with smallpox in Berkeley, Gloucestershire in 1757, and only developed a mild case of smallpox, and immunity which saved his life from later epidemics. His name was Edward Jenner. He would devote his life to finding a better and safer response. He had heard tales that dairymaids were protected after they had suffered from cowpox, and started to inoculate people with it to make them immune from smallpox. The Latin word for cow is *vacca*, and *vaccinus* means of or from a cow, so Jenner called his new procedure 'vaccination'. He promoted it relentlessly and in 1800 vaccination had reached most European countries.

The germ theory of disease was an enormous breakthrough that made more focused measures possible. It seemed impossible that microorganisms, things that were too small to see, could be a cause of disease and death. But natural experiments began to change the prevailing view. In the mid-nineteenth century, the Hungarian obstetrician Ignaz Semmelweis famously noticed a high incidence of puerperal fever among pregnant women who delivered with the help of physicians, whereas it was much lower among those helped by midwives. He connected this with the fact that the physicians had often come straight from autopsies, and made them wash their hands with chlorinated lime water, which reduced maternal deaths by almost ninety per cent.

New microscopes had made it possible to see microorganisms. Especially important was the achromatic microscope, invented by Joseph Jackson Lister. The French chemist Louis Pasteur showed that microorganisms could spoil milk and wine, and invented a technique to prevent bacterial contamination – pasteurization. He also developed vaccines for rabies and anthrax.

As knowledge about microorganisms began to take hold, it gave an extra urgency to attempts to improve sanitation and water supplies and vaccination became routine. The knowledge about germs in itself also made people change behaviour. Until the theory was established, hotels did not change bed linens between guests, doctors used instruments that weren't sterilized, and water was not always boiled to kill bacteria. It took time before health personnel were convinced to wash their hands and sterilize equipment, but when it happened it had an amazing effect on maternal death. In countries that hold data, such as Sweden and Finland, around 1,000 mothers died per 100,000 child births in 1800. Those are shocking numbers: the mother died in every hundredth childbirth. Since mothers gave birth much more often than today, this would have been a regular occurrence in a family. And 100 years later, the number was still around 500 per 100,000 births. But after the Second World War it fell below 100 in high-income countries, and today it is below ten. In Britain, the rate fell from 458 to nine between 1935 and 2015.[13]

The increase in agricultural production meant that more calories were available, but at least as important was the reduction of infection among children, which helped them to benefit from that nutrition, rather than wasting it fighting fevers, diarrhoea and infection. Western Europe and its offshoots moved from the Age of Pestilence and Famine to the Age of Receding Pandemics. Life expectancy, which had been fairly stable for tens of thousands of years, jumped by twenty years in the five decades following 1880. This was totally unprecedented. But as science and knowledge spread to other parts of the world, and as they got richer, the same thing happened there.

Avoiding bacteria is beneficial, but it is even better to be able to kill them off. Otherwise anything that breaks through the skin, our first barrier against disease, can be lethal, even something as innocuous as a scraped knee. Before penicillin, hospitals were full of people dying from tiny cuts and children dying from scarlet fever and infections.

'When I woke up just after dawn on September 28, 1928, I certainly didn't plan to revolutionise all medicine by discovering the world's first antibiotic, or bacteria killer,' the Scottish biologist Alexander Fleming once said, 'but I suppose that was exactly what I did.'

Fleming had been studying the properties of staphylococci and when he left his (famously untidy) laboratory for the August holiday, he stacked the specimens on a bench. When Fleming returned, he realized that one culture of staphylococci had been contaminated with a fungus, which had killed the surrounding bacteria. 'That's funny,' he remarked.

It was. That day, he discovered antibiotics and it became possible for others to develop the 'wonder drug' penicillin. At the end of the Second World War it saved 3,000 Allied soldiers on Normandy Beach from deadly gangrene on D-Day. Antibiotics turned small but life-threatening infections into trivial conditions, almost eradicated amputations and made modern surgery and organ transplantation possible. At the same time, penicillin helped battle ancient diseases such as the plague, tuberculosis and syphilis. It has saved the lives of millions and millions of people.

After the Second World War, the richest countries were well on their way to solving the problem of early death. Since the late nineteenth century, infant mortality had been reduced from around ten to twenty-five dead per hundred births, to two to five per hundred births.[14] Life expectancy in western Europe in the 1950s was sixty-eight years, up from thirty-six in the 1850s. But life expectancy in the world's poor and middle-income countries was still where it had been in the richest countries in the late nineteenth century. In sub-Saharan Africa it was thirty-eight years. More than 100 countries lost more than a fifth of all children before their first birthday.

But at this time the ideas and the technology that had saved Western children began to spread to other regions as well. Penicillin became widely accessible and institutions such as UNICEF and the WHO launched vaccination campaigns against tuberculosis, diphtheria, measles and polio. The percentage of the world's infants vaccinated against diphtheria, pertussis and tetanus increased from one-fifth to four-fifths between 1970 and 2006.[15] Smallpox was defeated in country after country until 8 May 1980 when the World Health Assembly announced: 'The world and all its people have won freedom from smallpox, which was the most devastating disease sweeping in epidemic form through many countries since earliest times, leaving death, blindness and disfigurement in its wake.'[16]

Humanity has now also come close to eradicating the polio virus, which can result in muscle weakness, paralysis and even death. After a global vaccination campaign by the WHO, UNICEF and the Rotary Foundation, the number of annual cases has been reduced by more than ninety-nine per cent since 1988, from 350,000 cases to 416. Vaccination has also reduced the deaths of newborns and mothers from neonatal tetanus by ninety-six per cent since 1988.

The next big killer that may be beaten is malaria, which was endemic to almost every country in the world in 1900 and killed about two million a year. At that stage, rich countries drained swamps and ditched marshy areas to remove breeding sites for the mosquitoes that carry the parasite. This and the widespread use of insecticides such as DDT eradicated malaria in more than 100 countries. After a recent push by the Gates Foundation and other groups, there is now a chance that malaria could be beaten globally in the next few decades. Between 2000 and 2015 malaria death rates around the world have reduced by around half, declining fastest among children. According to the WHO, this has averted 6.2 million deaths.

This has happened thanks to bed nets treated with insecticides, indoor residual spraying and artemisinin-based combination therapy. Africa is the region most burdened by malaria, but progress has been quick. The population sleeping under mosquito nets has increased from less than two per cent to about fifty-five per cent. Malaria mortality among children under five has declined by seventy-one per cent.[17]

For present generations, HIV/AIDS seems like a modern version of the plague. It spreads silently, kills millions and foxes our attempts to defeat it. But if it appears unassailable, that is only because we now trust medicine to come up with rapid responses to all ills. As Angus Deaton writes, the discovery of the HIV virus, the deduction of its means of transmission and the development of chemotherapy to treat it has been 'extraordinarily rapid by historical standards'.[18] AIDS has killed almost forty million people worldwide, but modern science has now turned a certain death sentence into a chronic condition. New

HIV infections have fallen by thirty-five per cent since 2000, and the number of AIDS-related deaths has fallen by forty-two per cent since 2006.[19]

The grave Ebola outbreak in West Africa in 2014–15 shows how fast science, health workers and the general population can now respond to a health crisis, thanks to the co-ordination of information and research. In late 2014, America's Centers for Disease Control and Prevention warned that there could be 1.4 million cases in Liberia and Sierra Leone alone in early 2015 without effective intervention. But people changed their behaviour, they turned to safe burials and cases were isolated. The total number of cases turned out to be no more than 30,000. An Ebola vaccine has proved successful, so the disease should be even less destructive if there is another outbreak.

Nonetheless, millions of people still die because of geography. In almost forty countries, more than ten per cent of children die before their fifth birthday, because of diseases that rich countries eradicated a long time ago. Nearly eight million people die every year because of lower respiratory infections, diarrhoea, tuberculosis, and childhood diseases such as whooping cough and diphtheria.

But the overall direction is remarkably positive. In 1960, almost a quarter of all children born in low- and middle-income countries died before their fifth birthday. Since then, it has been reduced from 232 to forty-seven deaths per 1,000 live births. The number of infant deaths has been reduced from 154 to thirty-five per 1,000 live births from 1960 to 2015.[20]

Maternal mortality is still very high in developing countries, but in the last twenty-five years, it has dropped sharply. Between 1990 and 2015, maternal deaths per 100,000 births have declined from 435 to 242 and most of that reduction occurred after the year 2000. The ratio has declined by almost half in Africa, the Middle East and Latin America, and by around two-thirds in South and East Asia. The lifetime risk of dying while giving birth was reduced from 6.1 to 2.8% in sub-Saharan Africa, and from 2.6 to 0.5% in South Asia. This is the result of basic hygiene, access to safe water and attendance by health personnel, which was the case at fifty-nine per cent of the births worldwide in 1990 and at seventy-one per cent today.[21]

One of the people responsible for saving the most lives in history is Maurice Hilleman. He originally intended to become a manager at a J. C. Penney store, but apparently did not have the right personality for retail. That was lucky for us, because he studied for a PhD in microbiology instead, got a job at Merck and went on to develop over twenty-five vaccines, including most of those now recommended to children.

The most important of these was the measles vaccine. Since the mid-1800s, measles is estimated to have killed about 200 million people. Several million died every year until a vaccine was made available in the early 1970s. Today, it results in around 100,000 deaths annually, a reduction of more than ninety-six per cent since the early 1980s. Similarly, leprosy, a disease that results in loss of feeling in parts of the extremities, has affected humanity for thousands of years. In the 1950s there were 10.5 million cases of leprosy, but the cure came in the form of three drugs invented in the 1960s. Today there are fewer than 200,000 chronic cases worldwide.

One of the great global health triumphs of the past few decades is also one of the cheapest – Oral Hydration Therapy. In the 1970s one in ten children in poor countries died of dehydration caused by diarrhoea before the age of five. Scientists and doctors had searched for an antidote for a long time, and had suggested everything from bananas to carrot soup. An especially promising solution was a mixture of salt and sugar in water, and its promise was demonstrated during a cholera outbreak in Indian and Bangladeshi refugee camps in the early 1970s. Three thousand patients were treated and their mortality rate was reduced by almost ninety per cent. Oral Hydration Therapy, at a cost of only a few cents a dose, quickly got worldwide attention, and is now estimated to save the lives of around one million children annually. The UK medical journal *Lancet* described it as 'potentially the most important medical advance of this century'.[22]

The result of such life-saving technologies has been the quickest extension of life spans the world has ever seen. Child mortality in developing countries – the proportion of children dying before the age of five – has declined from 240 to sixty-eight per thousand born, a reduction by seventy-two per cent.[23] As we saw in Kenya, several countries recorded increases in life expectancy of more than one year *every year* for more than a decade. After having lived through a decade, the average person in those countries could expect to have more years left than they'd had at the beginning of the decade. Between 1950 and 2011, life expectancy in Asia increased from forty-two to seventy years, in Latin America from fifty to seventy-four years, and even in Africa, despite the disaster of HIV/AIDS, life expectancy increased more than it had ever done, from thirty-seven to fifty-seven years.

This is the reason why we have experienced an unprecedented growth in global population, which many in the West saw as a huge threat in the 1970s and 1980s. Between 1950 and 2011 world population grew from 2.5 to seven billion.

This did not happen because people in poor countries started breeding like rabbits, as people sometimes assumed; it happened because they stopped dying like flies. But it did not take long until families started adapting. As parents came to realize that their children were less likely to die young, they stopped having as many babies. In 1950, the average woman in less developed regions had 6.2 children over her lifetime, whereas today she has no more than 2.6. In Asia, some attribute this fertility decline to brutal policies like China's one-child policy, but fertility fell much further among the Chinese in Taiwan and by exactly the same rate in Thailand. Women don't suffer through as many pregnancies, and parents are spared the agony of having to see their children dying.

The wealthier a country is, the healthier it is. Variation in income can explain over seventy per cent of the variation in infant and child mortality. No country with an income per capita above $10,000 has an infant mortality rate above two per cent. Richer people can invest more in sanitation and water facilities, and can afford food and medicine. But it is not just that humanity is getting richer, so it can afford a better standard of living. That is not even the major cause. Even more important is that a decent standard of living is getting much cheaper.

Health indicators for a given income level are improving all the time. A country with a per capita income of $1,000 had an infant mortality rate of twenty per hundred births in 1900. A country at exactly the same income level in 2000 had an infant mortality rate of only seven per hundred births. So even if a country had not experienced any economic growth in a hundred years, infant mortality would have been reduced by two-thirds. A country with a GDP per capita of $3,000 today has the same life expectancy as would have been predicted for a hypothetical country with a GDP per capita of $30,000 in 1870. This is the great health story of our time: low prices for a good life.[24]

It is a result of globalization, which makes it easier for countries to use the knowledge and technology that it took generations and vast sums of money to generate. It is difficult to develop cellular technology, the germ theory of disease or a vaccine against measles, but it is easy to use it once someone else has. The infrastructure that has been created for trade and communication also makes it easier to transmit ideas, science and technology across borders, in a virtuous cycle.[25]

Interestingly, even though there is a strong relationship between health and wealth, it is difficult to find a relationship between health and recent growth rates. The economist William Easterly has shown that the correlation between a country's health indicators and its own growth rate is not as strong as the correlation between its health indicators and global growth. In this era of globalization, the most important factor behind a country's success is the success of other countries. Even a country such as Haiti, which is one of very few countries that is poorer today than it was in the 1950s, has reduced its infant mortality rate by almost two-thirds. Haiti actually has lower infant mortality than the richest countries on the planet had in 1900.

It is natural that the increase in life expectancy slows down after such amazing gains, as diseases move out of the bowels and chests of infants and into the arteries of the elderly. When children's lives are saved it has a huge effect on life expectancy. When a child is saved and goes on to live to old age, their life is extended by several decades. Mortality among children is now so low that progress mostly takes place among older adults, and that has a more muted effect on life expectancy at birth. Eradicating cancer completely would be an amazing accomplishment, but it would only increase life expectancy in rich countries by a few years.

Despite this, life expectancy keeps increasing even in the richest countries. Even though it was close to seventy years in the 1950s, it has increased by another decade since then. This is a completely new phenomenon in humanity's history. In the 1970s, cheap medication to lower blood pressure spread from the United States, and so did other ways of treating heart disease. This reduced mortality from cardiovascular disease by around two-thirds in most Western countries, and is now reaching poorer countries as well. That people smoke less is also important, because it is a cause of lung cancer and cardiovascular disease. Perhaps it is time to start talking about a fourth stage of mortality: *the Age of Receding Degenerative and Man-Made Diseases.*

People have to die from something, and if they don't fall at the first hurdle, there will be more people to fall at the second and third. This may have disguised some of the progress that has been made against cancer in the last few decades. When fewer die from cardiovascular diseases, many more should die from cancer. Since this has not been the case, it shows that improvement in the treatment of cancer has already had a great effect, even though this has been much more costly than the prevention of cardiovascular disease. In almost every age group, fewer get cancer. The incidence rate in the US has fallen by about 0.6% per year since 1994. Rates of cancer deaths have fallen twenty-two per cent in the last two decades.[26]

What does the future hold in store? Nothing is certain. New pandemics can appear at any time. At some point, an influenza virus will likely mutate into a form that is sufficiently deadly to take a terrible toll on humanity, like the Spanish flu did in 1918, when it probably killed more than fifty million people. On the other hand, the scientific and technological defences at our disposal are of an entirely different kind, and more people than ever can contribute.

Following the H1N1 flu in 2009, a totally new version of the virus from 1918, we saw the quickest response to a pandemic in history. The internet made it possible to track the outbreak and facilitated co-operation between institutions, scientists and health workers around the world. After American scientists got a sample of the virus from a patient in mid-April 2009, the gene sequencing was done in just one day. Within a week the full H1N1 virus genome was published online, for the whole world to use. This made it possible for test developers around the world to modify existing tests and find new cases. Before the month was over, new test kits were sent to clinical and public health laboratories.

At the same time, drug companies used this information, new cell culture technologies and other new breakthroughs to start working on vaccines. In June 2009 the WHO declared that H1N1 was a pandemic. Just three months later several manufacturers had already completed vaccine development and started producing it. By December, over fifty countries had started vaccine programmes.

There is no guarantee that life expectancy will keep on increasing. HIV/AIDS led to a sudden plunge in life expectancy in several African countries that is rarely matched even in war. Zimbabwe and Botswana lost more than fifteen years in life expectancy. In the years after the planned economy collapsed, life expectancy in Russia fell by five years. On the other hand, life expectancy in Africa is now seven years higher than it was *before* HIV/AIDS took its toll, and life expectancy in Russia is now higher than it ever was under communism, so there is a case to be made that life expectancy moves in a general direction, even though we also see obstacles and even temporary reversals.[27] Life expectancy is also, in many ways, a conservative estimate. It is a measure of the time that the average newborn can expect to live if we see no further improvement in health, so it doesn't take into account any further progress in the extension of life spans.

Some say that we have reached the limits of what is possible, that life spans can't increase much further. But they have said this before, again and again, and they have always been wrong. In 1928, when US life expectancy was fifty-seven years, the statistician Louis Dublin calculated that the ultimate possibility was sixty-five years. Since he did not have numbers for New Zealand, he did not know that this cap had already been surpassed by the women there. Another research team repeated the exercise in 1990, and settled on a limit of eighty-five years. That was reached by Japanese females in 1996.[28]

A wonderful paper by Jim Oeppen and James Vaupel looks at the forecasts of experts, including the United Nations and the World Bank, who have repeatedly asserted that life expectancy is approaching a ceiling. The paper concludes that those ceilings have always been broken, on average five years after the estimate was published. Oeppen and Vaupel point out that female life expectancy in the record-holding country has risen for an amazing 160 years at a steady pace of almost three months per year, and there is no end in sight. The apparent levelling off in some countries is an artefact of laggards catching up and leaders falling behind. Amazingly, there is not a single country that hasn't seen improvements in infant and child mortality since 1950.[29]

Angus Deaton finds the optimistic argument more compelling: 'ever since people rebelled against authority in the Enlightenment, and set about using the force of reason to make their lives better, they have found a way to do so, and there is little doubt that they will continue to win victories against the forces of death.'[30]

As people got healthier and secured a stable supply of food, they could work harder and better. As life expectancy increased, skills could be built up for longer and were put to better use. Smaller families meant that each child got a better start in life and a longer education. Humanity could finally start defeating that ancient scourge, poverty.

4

POVERTY

[P]overty has no causes. Only prosperity has causes.

Jane Jacobs[1]

Why are some people poor?

That is the wrong question.

We do not need an explanation for poverty, because that is the starting point for everybody. Poverty is what you have until you create wealth. It is easy to forget the dreadful circumstances of our ancestors' lives even in the richest countries. The accepted definition of poverty in a country like France was very simple: if you could afford to buy bread to survive another day, you were not poor. In hard times, towns were filled with armies of poor, dressed in rags, begging for something to eat.

Even in normal times the margins were exceedingly narrow. The French economic historian Fernand Braudel has found that estate inventories compiled following the deaths of ordinary Europeans before the eighteenth century 'testify almost exclusively to universal poverty'. This is what the assembled effects of an elderly person, with an entire working life behind them, would look like: 'a few old clothes, a stool, a table, a bench, the planks of a bed, sacks filled with straw. Official reports from Burgundy between the 16th and 18th centuries are full of "references to people [sleeping on straw] ... with no bed or furniture" who were only separated "from the pigs by a screen".[2]

An inquiry in 1564 into Pescara on the Adriatic, a not particularly poor town with a fortress and a garrison, found that three-quarters of the families in the town lived in make-shift shelters. In wealthy Genoa, poor people sold themselves as galley slaves every winter. In Paris the very poor were chained together in pairs and forced to do the hard work of cleaning the drains. In England, the poor had to work in workhouses to get relief, where they worked long hours for almost no pay. Some were instructed to crush dog, horse and cattle bones for use as fertilizer, until an inspection of a workhouse in 1845 showed that hungry paupers were fighting over the rotting bones to suck out the marrow.

Despite a few ups and downs, humanity had experienced almost no economic development until the early nineteenth century. According to the rough estimates by the economist Angus Maddison, GDP per capita – the value of goods and services per person – increased by only fifty per cent between the year 1 CE and 1820, not enough for people to experience any increase in wealth during their own lifetime.[3]

Europe was a little more privileged than other continents, but in 1820, GDP per capita in the richest countries of western Europe was the equivalent of around $1,500 to $2,000 (in 1990 dollars, adjusted for purchasing power). This is less than in present-day Mozambique and Pakistan. Even if all incomes had been perfectly equally distributed (which they certainly weren't), it would have meant a life of extreme deprivation for everybody. The average world citizen lived in abject misery, as poor as the average person in Haiti, Liberia and Zimbabwe today.

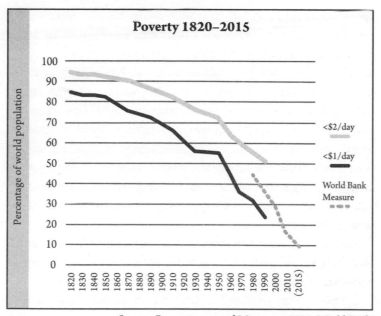

Sources: Bourguignon and Morrisson 2002; World Bank,
PovcalNet; Cruz, Foster, Quillin and Schellekens 2015.[4]

In the early nineteenth century, poverty rates even in the
richest countries were higher than in the poor countries today.
In the United States, Britain and France, around forty to fifty
per cent of the population lived in what we now call extreme
poverty, a rate that you have to go to sub-Saharan Africa to find
today. In Scandinavia, Austria-Hungary, Germany and Spain
around sixty to seventy per cent were extremely poor.[5]
Homelessness was a common phenomenon. Between ten and
twenty per cent of the European and American population was
classified as paupers and vagrants by officials.[6]

Until then, the dominant economic school, Mercantilism,
taught that poverty was necessary. It was considered the only

way to incentivize people to work hard, and it was thought that only low wages could reduce the cost of production so that a country could remain competitive. If the poor got a raise, they would leave the job and end up in the alehouse, according to many thinkers of the time. The Scottish economist Adam Smith, the arch-enemy of the Mercantilists, thought that this was wrong, arguing that higher wages could in fact make people work more and that 'no society can surely be flourishing and happy, of which the far greater part of the members are poor and miserable.'[7] The ideas of Smith and other Enlightenment thinkers developed a growing respect for the hard-working poor.

By then, the Industrial Revolution was taking off in Europe, starting in England, a country where government control of the economy had been scaled back and the élites did not try to resist new technologies like they did in other places. A new openness to experiments and technological applications of scientific discoveries improved production methods that had stayed almost the same for a thousand years. Spinning and weaving was mechanized and the stationary steam engine made it possible to power production in the cities, without water wheels. As innovation produced unprecedented productivity increases, the production value of every worker increased, and so did incomes. Between 1820 and 1850, when the population grew by a third, workers' real earnings rose by almost 100 per cent.[8] If earlier trends had continued, it would have taken the average person 2,000 years to double his income, but the English achieved this in only thirty years.

Karl Marx thought that capitalism would make the rich richer and the poor poorer. If someone was to gain, someone else had to lose in the free market. The middle class would become proletarians, and the proletarians would starve. But when Marx died in 1883, the average Englishman was three times richer than he was when Marx was born, in 1818. By 1900, extreme poverty in England had already been reduced by three-quarters, to around ten per cent. Never before had the human race experienced anything like it.

After thousands of years when no country experienced a sustained growth in per capita income, the West started growing by more than one per cent per capita annually from 1820 to 1870, a rate that increased to 1.6% from 1870 to 1913, and picked up again after the two World Wars. Since 1820, per capita GDP in the Western world has increased more than fifteen-fold. In the early 1900s, extreme poverty had been reduced to around ten to twenty per cent in western Europe and in North America. The fact that we worked smarter, with better technology, also made it possible to reduce working hours. The average working week for Americans has been reduced by twenty-five hours since 1860. Add to this the fact that we also start work later in life, retire earlier and live longer after retirement. If we valued the extra leisure hours at the average wage, GDP per capita would rise by around 120%.[9]

This was the first Great Ascent from poverty and human deprivation, as the United Nation's Development Programme (UNDP) has memorably described it.[10] This ascent was almost complete in the 1950s when extreme poverty was eradicated in almost all western European countries. At this point, the second Great Ascent began. It started in East Asia, where countries such as Japan, South Korea, Taiwan, Hong Kong and Singapore integrated into the global economy and proved to the world that development was possible for 'developing countries'. And it picked up speed when the world's two giants, China and India, decided to start opening their economies in 1979 and 1991 respectively. The progress of the Asian economies is unprecedented. Since 1950, India's GDP per capita has grown five-fold, Japan's eleven-fold and China's almost twenty-fold.

This was not what the world had expected. In the 1960s and 1970s the Swedish author Lasse Berg and the photographer Stig Karlsson visited several Asian countries, documenting misery and warning about impending disaster. They had read what the experts had written about a hopeless continent, where they expected to find overpopulation, endless war and famines. They had learned from the economist Gunnar Myrdal, the authority on Asia in those days, that China was too chaotic to function, Malaysia had too much ethnic division and the South Koreans did not have a work ethic because of their religion. Berg and Karlsson saw what they expected to see, and thought that the worst was yet to come: 'Doomsday was approaching, in one way or the other.'[11]

But in the 1990s they returned to the same places and villages and found a continent of hope. 'Nothing was the way I had expected,' Berg writes:

My Asia pulled through. Better clothes, more food, improved security. But above all, this revolution in people's minds. Where poverty used to be natural ('my parents were poor, I am poor, my children will be poor – it has always been that way and always will') it was now considered outrageous, unjust, unsustainable by the poor themselves. It was the same in every country: India, China, Japan, Indonesia, Malaysia, South Korea etc. Less poverty, rapidly increasing life expectancy, greater openness, freedom and knowledge. Things had turned out much better than I thought possible.[12]

In India they found that even the poorest villages no longer smelled of urine and faeces, and mud huts had started to be replaced by brick buildings, keeping the heat in and the insects out. They were wired up for electricity and had television sets. When they showed young Indians what things looked like on their last visit, the young people refused to believe it was the same place. Could things really have been that miserable here? When Berg returned again in 2010, the transformation had gone even further. There were motorcycles and big markets and all the villagers walked around with mobile phones. Now even the poorest live in brick buildings with iron bars in front of the windows. The casual observer would say that this means that crime is up. Berg points out that it means that even the poor now own something worth stealing.

The key to Asia's development was its integration into the global economy. Better transport and communication technologies and more openness to trade and investment in recent years have made it possible for low- and middle-income countries to prosper. Even poor countries that opened their economies could find a niche in a free trade world by producing simple but labour-intensive goods such as clothes, toys and electronics. This led to a constant upgrading of skills and production, so that they became better at more qualified, technology-intensive production, and eventually knowledge-intensive production, such as finance, law, PR, research and education. This in turn gave other poor countries an opportunity to step into the old labour-intensive niche. This is why East Asian economies have been likened to a flock of geese. From their different positions in the flock, they have all moved forward to better positions, step by step.

In no place has this happened on a larger scale than in China, a country where three generations around a dinner table can

tell the whole rags-to-riches story, from hunger and subsistence agriculture to programming computers and making
cosmetics. At the start of the 1980s the city of Guangzhou, in
the south-east Chinese province of Guangdong, had two buildings of more than ten floors. This was one of the poorer provinces of a desperately poor China, with neither capital nor
resources for development. But farmers and villagers had
started small businesses and began to improve production. As
we saw in the case of the farmers in Xiaogang, they often did so
without official recognition, but it inspired the leadership to
think differently.

In its efforts to raise the country out of its abysmal poverty,
the Chinese communist party learned from the Asian 'tiger'
economies of South Korea, Taiwan, Hong Kong and Singapore,
but also from local experiments with private farming and town-
ship enterprises. So it allowed special economic zones in
Guangdong from 1980, which were exempt from the rules of
the command economy. Production was mostly based on
market forces, international investments and technologies
were welcome, and they could engage in international trade.
Business there combined investments from Hong Kong and
Taiwan, received workers from northern provinces and sold to
Western markets.

Although better wages inspired workers to move to the new
industrial towns, this created new problems. Two local labour
representatives tell me that there is an old Chinese proverb:
'Everything is good back home. Everything is difficult when
you migrate.' The lack of formal property rights means that
migrants can't sell before they move and when they return to
their home towns local authorities have often appropriated
their land. The *hukou* household registration system that is

currently under reform means that migrants lose their automatic rights to health care and free schooling. Attempts to organize in trade unions are struck down by the government.

But rapidly increased productivity also raised wages and improved labour conditions. Guangdong became a manufacturing and export powerhouse and inspired the rest of the country to go in the same direction. The result was astonishing growth and poverty reduction. Almost nine in ten Chinese lived in extreme poverty in 1981. Only one in ten do today. Walking today along the gently lit and scrupulously clean quayside on the Pearl River, one sees work in progress on new skyscrapers long after office hours. The two high-rise blocks now have company. Probably two new buildings were completed during the week I stayed there. There are now more than 100 skyscrapers across the city.

After China came the other giant, India. One Indian economist I met, Parth Shah, said that the country learned from Taiwan and South Korea, but obviously also from its big neighbour, China: 'we saw that they actually changed their model and they did succeed in what they had done and it was time for India to learn the lesson.'

This was important in 1991, when a debt-fuelled boom crashed and foreign exchange reserves had been reduced to such a point that India could barely finance three weeks' worth of imports. The crisis caused Finance Minister Manmohan Singh to stand up in Parliament and quote the nineteenth-century romantic Victor Hugo: 'Nothing is more powerful than an idea whose time has come.' The idea was to dismantle the protectionism and planned economy that had held India in poverty since independence in 1947. License requirements were removed, tariff barriers were reduced and the Indians got more freedom to start businesses and compete with the old monopolies. What used to be known as the 'Hindu rate of growth' – a growth rate slower than population growth – is history. Since the reforms, average incomes have increased by 7.5% a year, which means that they double in a decade.

The transition can be seen even among the *dalits* in India, who occupy the lowest level of the caste system. Making up nearly a quarter of the population, they were denied an education and given the worst and the dirtiest jobs, cleaning toilets, flaying and tanning skins, and handling the dead. Since this exposed them to filth and germs, it became taboo for others even to be close to them, and so they became known as 'untouchables'. They were forced to live in ghettoes and could not even enter temples, but had to pray from outside.

But one benefit of urbanization and liberalization is that the markets care more about what people can do and at what price, rather than where they come from or their family history. When businesses were exposed to competition it suddenly became costly to grant favours to the upper castes and to discriminate against good workers just because they were *dalits*.

In a documentary that I made in 2015, *India Awakes*, we profiled one *dalit*, Madhusudan Rao, who moved from his village to Hyderabad looking for a better life. There he overheard a contractor scolding an employee for failing to supply enough workers to dig trenches for telecom cables. Madhusudan stepped up and offered to find twenty-five workers by 10 p.m. that night. He borrowed money from his sister to hire a truck, went out into the countryside and found whatever men were willing and able. The contractor was satisfied and the workers were paid immediately. Madhusudan earned more money that day than he had seen in his entire life.

Since then he moved on in the sector and has formed a construction company with 350 workers. 'When I'm hiring employees, I am not seeing any caste. I'm seeing if they're talented.' Madhusudan has moved into a posh housing estate previously reserved for higher castes and he has been able to give his extended family a comfortable life. His mother-in-law is overjoyed: 'My son-in-law should have God's blessings. If one tree grows big, it becomes a shelter for many plants and creatures, and gives shade to many. This is also like that. If one in the family is well off, he or she will be able to help others.'

Indian data show that, between 1993–4 and 2011–12, poverty declined by almost twenty-four per cent, but the poverty ratio of *dalits* declined even faster, by more than thirty-one per cent. We have more detailed data from two districts in India's biggest state, Uttar Pradesh, between 1990 and 2008. There, the proportion of *dalit* households that own electric fans (which presupposes access to electricity) increased from three to forty-nine per cent and the proportion who lived in brick houses increased from an average of twenty-eight to eighty per cent.

The material improvement of *dalits* has gone hand in hand with the social empowerment of the poor. The practice of separate seating at upper-caste weddings has declined from seventy-five to thirteen per cent and the proportion of non-*dalits* who accept food and water at *dalit* households has increased from three to sixty per cent. Chandra Bhan Prasad, now an adviser to the Dalit Indian Chamber of Commerce, once joined Maoist insurrections to fight the caste system; now he thinks 'capitalism is changing caste much faster'.[13]

The effect on self-esteem and prejudice is crucial since poverty is not just a material condition, but also a psychological one, leading to 'loss, grief, anguish, worry, over-thinking, madness, frustration, anger, alienation, humiliation, shame, loneliness, depression, anxiety and fear'.[14] In a study based on interviews with 60,000 poor men and women from over sixty countries, the World Bank documented the experience of poverty. As we might expect, the poor talked about the lack of food, clothing and shelter, but they also talked about humiliating treatment meted out by the rich or by the government, about corruption, crime, violence and a general sense of insecurity. Some talked about a lack of self-confidence, which meant that they hardly travelled out of the community and often stayed in the house all day.[15]

China and India are the biggest countries that are beating poverty, but they are representative of what has being going on in the era of globalization. Between 1960 and the end of the 1990s rich countries still grew faster than poor on average. Only thirty per cent of developing countries grew faster than the United States. In 1997 Lant Pritchett, then chief economist of the World Bank, published the paper 'Divergence, big time', a title that left little to the imagination. He wrote that divergence in living standards 'is the dominant feature of modern economic history' and that periods when poor countries rapidly approach the rich were 'historically rare'.[16]

But since then, that is exactly what has happened. Between 2000 and 2011, ninety per cent of developing countries have grown faster than the US, and they have done it on average by three per cent annually.[17] In just a decade, per capita income in the world's low- and middle-income countries has doubled.

According to some statisticians, 28 March 2012 was a big day for humanity. It was the first day in modern history that developing countries were responsible for more than half of global GDP, up from thirty-eight per cent ten years earlier.[18] This convergence makes sense. If people have freedom and access to knowledge, technology and capital, there is no reason why they shouldn't be able to produce as much as people anywhere else. A country with a fifth of the world's population should produce around a fifth of its wealth. That has not been the case for centuries, because many parts of the world were held back by oppression, colonialism, socialism and protectionism. But these have now diminished, and a revolution in transport and communication technology makes it easier to take advantage of a global division of labour, and use technologies and knowledge that it took other countries generations and vast sums of money to develop.

This has resulted in the greatest poverty reduction the world has ever seen. The World Bank categorizes a person as living in 'extreme poverty' if he or she can't consume more than $1.90 per day at 2005 prices. The numbers are adjusted for inflation and local purchasing power, so (at least in theory) this should represent exactly the same standard of living whether we are talking about Brazil or Burkina Faso, in 1981 or 2015. This extreme poverty line is the average of the national poverty lines of the fifteen poorest developing countries, so it is much lower than the poverty lines you hear about in the UK or the USA.

We have detailed statistics in this area stretching back to 1981, based on more than a thousand regularly updated surveys of nationally representative households in almost all low- and middle-income countries. In 1981, fifty-four per cent of the developing world population lived in extreme poverty, according to the World Bank. This already marks an historic achievement. According to an ambitious attempt to measure poverty over the long run, with a $2 a day threshold for extreme poverty, adjusted for purchasing power in 1985, ninety-four per cent of the world's population lived in extreme poverty in 1820, eighty-two per cent in 1910 and seventy-two per cent in 1950.[19]

But in the last few decades things have really begun to change. Between 1981 and 2015 the proportion of low- and middle-income countries suffering from extreme poverty was reduced from fifty-four per cent to twelve per cent. Most people in poverty lived in Asia, and that is also where we have seen the greatest progress. In South Asia extreme poverty was reduced from fifty-eight to fourteen per cent, and remarkably, in East Asia and the Pacific it was reduced from eighty-one to four per cent.

Table 2. Extreme poverty, percentage of population, <$1.90/day

	1981	1990	1999	2010	2015
Europe and Central Asia	–	1.9	7.8	2.8	1.7
Latin America	23.9	17.8	13.9	6.4	5.6
East Asia	80.6	60.6	37.4	11.2	4.1
South Asia	58.1	50.6	–	27.2	13.5
Sub-Saharan Africa	–	56.8	58	46.1	35.2
Developing world	53.9	44.4	34.3	19	11.9
World	44.3	37.1	29.1	16.3	9.6

Source: World Bank, *PovcalNet*; Cruz et al. 2015, p. 6. 2015 is a projection.

Don't pay too much attention to the specific numbers in table 2. I almost feel guilty for providing you with decimals, because it gives the numbers a false sense of reliability. We are nowhere near that accurate. We have to rely on interviews with a selection of households about what they have consumed over a given period, and then we extrapolate from the survey data to the underlying population. In every step of the process there are problems – who do we reach, who do we miss, do people remember what they consumed, are they honest, have we adjusted for local prices and inflation in the right way? So we have to be cautious. But any errors won't always run in the same direction, and the fact that the numbers point to such an incredibly strong trend tells us something. By all our best estimates, global poverty has been reduced by more than one percentage point annually for three decades.

At the same time, global population has grown dramatically, so it could be that the number of poor has grown even though the proportion is declining. But nobody would claim that unemployment is rising in a society where the unemployment rate has halved from ten to five per cent, only because its population has slightly more than doubled over the same period. It would be appropriate here to consider the philosopher John Rawls's thought experiment about the 'veil of ignorance': if you had to choose a society to live in but did not know what your social or economic position would be, you would probably choose the society with the lowest proportion (not the lowest numbers) of poor, because this is the best judgement of the life of an average citizen.[20]

In fact, it doesn't matter what we focus on when it comes to recent poverty data. For the first time in world history, even the absolute number of poor is being reduced. At the Millennium Summit of the United Nations in 2000, the world's countries set the goal of halving the 1990 incidence of extreme poverty by 2015. This was met five years ahead of the deadline. Even though world population grew by more than two billion between 1990 and 2015, the number of people who live in extreme poverty was reduced by more than 1.25 billion people. This means that extreme poverty was reduced by more than fifty million every year and almost 138,000 people every day over twenty-five years. If it takes you twenty minutes to read this chapter, almost another 2,000 people will have risen out of poverty.

This marks a historic rupture. For the first time, poverty is not growing just because population is growing. Because of this reduction, the number of people in extreme poverty is now slightly less than it was in 1820. Then it was around one billion, while today it is 700 million. If this does not sound like progress, you should note that in 1820, the world only had around sixty million people who did *not* live in extreme poverty. Today more than 6.5 billion people do not live in extreme poverty. So the risk of living in poverty has been reduced from ninety-four per cent to less than eleven per cent.[21]

There are many theories on how to fight poverty, and global institutions wrestle with the question of how to make growth 'pro-poor'. But it seems like the best way of making growth pro-poor is to make it high and keep it high. A study of 118 countries over four decades shows that almost all the income growth for the poorest in society has been led by average growth in those countries, rather than changes in income distribution. Seventy-seven per cent of the national variation in growth in incomes of the poorest forty per cent is due to growth in average incomes, and sixty-two per cent of the variation in incomes of the poorest fifth. So the amount of wealth being generated has a greater effect than its distribution.

It is important to understand the difference between this observation and the (often mythological) theory of 'trickle-down', which assumes that if only the rich get richer a few crumbs from their table will fall to the poorest. That is not what has happened. The poor are using the new opportunities to participate in modern patterns of production and trade and so make themselves rich, rather than waiting for someone else to do it.

The authors of the study conclude that economic growth is as close to a magic bullet as we are ever likely to see:

> So, if we are interested in 'shared prosperity', we have both good news and bad news. The good news is that institutions and policies that promote economic growth in general will on average raise incomes of the poor equiproportionally, thereby promoting 'shared prosperity'. The bad news is that, in choosing among macroeconomic policies, there is no robust evidence that certain policies are particularly 'pro-poor' or conducive to promoting 'shared prosperity' other than through their direct effects on overall economic growth.[22]

The continent that has lagged behind is sub-Saharan Africa, where the proportion in poverty has only declined slightly, and since its population has grown rapidly it means that there are now sixty million more in extreme poverty than there were in 1990. This reflects Africa's dismal growth record. After colonialism there was a period when the regional economy grew and the first steps towards industrialization were taken, but this was often based on protected companies that could not compete globally and were financed by debt. In the 1980s they suffered a debt crisis, and it has taken the region a long time to recover. Between 1981 and 2000, while the East Asian economy doubled in size, the African economy did not grow at all.

However, many African countries brought spending and inflation under control and began to improve the business climate. Many armed conflicts ended. Since then, growth has picked up strongly. A continent once synonymous with stagnation has grown by around five per cent annually since 2000. It is often assumed that this was just a commodity boom, but natural resources generated just a third of the growth, with the rest coming from sectors such as manufacturing, telecommunications, transportation and retail. In fact, African countries had similar growth rates regardless of whether they had natural resources to export or not. Extreme poverty in sub-Saharan Africa has been reduced from fifty-seven to thirty-five per cent since 1990. It is still a sign of widespread misery, but for the first time less than half of all Africans live in extreme poverty.

Life in the slums is also improving. According to the United Nations, slum-dwellers are rapidly gaining access to safe water, improved sanitation, durable housing and less crowded housing conditions. The proportion living in slums is also declining. It used to be said that with urbanization, half of new city-dwellers ended up in slums. That is no longer true. The proportion of the urban population in low- and middle-income countries living in slums has declined from forty-six per cent in 1990 to slightly less than thirty per cent in 2014. (At the same time the proportion of slum-dwellers increased dramatically in a few countries suffering from war or disastrous economic policies, such as Iraq and Zimbabwe.[23]) Just as Asia made the greatest progress against poverty, it reduced the proportion of slum-dwellers by the largest margin – in East Asia from forty-four to twenty-five per cent and in South Asia from fifty-seven to thirty-one per cent. But it was reduced in every region, including sub-Saharan Africa.

This doesn't mean we have seen the end of global poverty. Worldwide, more than 700 million people still live in extreme poverty, and many who have risen above the threshold are living in very vulnerable circumstances. Three-fifths of the world's extreme poor live in just five countries – Bangladesh, China, the Democratic Republic of Congo, India and Nigeria – so their policies have a disproportionate influence on the future of poverty. In twenty-six countries, more than forty per cent of the population live in extreme poverty. Except Bangladesh and Haiti, they are all in sub-Saharan Africa.

If countries continue to develop economically at the rate that they have in the past ten years, and income distribution remains the same, extreme poverty would fall to 5.6% of the developing world's population by 2030. If annual per capita consumption growth could reach four per cent in every country in the world, extreme poverty would be reduced to 3.5%. In East Asia the headcount would be at 0.3% and in South Asia 1.3%.[24]

There will be setbacks. Countries ravaged by war and epidemics have seen increased poverty and will do so in the future. But for the first time in world history extreme poverty is no longer the norm, and soon it will be a marginal phenomenon. As a result, multinational institutions are coming up with higher poverty lines that reflect higher ambitions. The World Bank has already changed the extreme poverty rate from $1 to $1.25 in 2008 and to $1.90 in 2015.

One result of the rapid growth in the developing world is a historically unique reduction in global inequality. Since 1820, when the Western world began to grow, the gaps between countries expanded. But since poor countries now grow faster than rich, we see convergence for the first time in modern economic history. A study from the Peterson Institute tries to measure inequality between all the world's citizens, by looking at inequality both between countries and within countries. Their conclusion is that global income inequality started to decline significantly at the turn of the century. According to their estimates, the Gini coefficient, a measure where 0 means everyone has the same wealth and 1 means one person has all the wealth, fell from 0.69 in 2003 to 0.65 in 2013. It is still extremely unequal, on a par with domestic inequality in South Africa, perhaps the most unequal country on the planet. But if the economic forecasts for the next two decades are anywhere close to the truth, the Gini will fall further, to 0.61 in 2035.[25]

We live in a remarkable time. Never before has the world seen such a dramatic poverty reduction. In a way, globalization is bigger than the Industrial Revolution. When the Western world began to industrialize around the year 1800, we were 200 million people and it took fifty years to double the average income. China and India have done the same thing with ten times more people, five times faster. So in a way, you could say that globalization is fifty times bigger than the Industrial Revolution.

This gigantic shift, with the emergence of a global middle class, will not just change consumption patterns; it will also change our lifestyles and our attitudes to life and other human beings. People with something precious to lose – a long, good life ahead – are not as willing to gamble everything for temporary gain. People who believe in the future also invest more in the future.

5

VIOLENCE

War appears to be as old as humanity, but peace is a modern invention.

Henry Maine, 1875[1]

With violent crime making the headlines every day, including the legacies of 9/11, Ukraine, Iraq, Afghanistan, Syria, the horrors of Islamic State and terror attacks on major European cities, we often think our era is especially plagued by violence. But psychologists have shown that we do not base such estimates on facts. Rather, we base these estimates on how easily we can recall examples.

We tend to think about new or current conflicts, like the civil war in Syria, but we forget the conflicts that ended in countries such as Sri Lanka, Angola and Chad during the same time. We often think of the recent wars in Afghanistan and Iraq, which have killed around 650,000 people, but we rarely talk about the conflicts in those countries between 1979 and 1989, which killed more than two million people.

War and violence used to be the natural state of humanity. The cognitive scientist Steven Pinker, on whose exhaustive research on the history of violence I draw heavily in this chapter, writes that the dramatic reduction in violence 'may be the most important thing that has ever happened in human history'.[2]

A tour through our cultural heritage, our myths, proverbs and even our language reveal how much of an everyday occurrence brutal violence was. The old folktales that the Grimm Brothers collected and retold in the early nineteenth century were filled with murder, cannibalism, mutilation and sexual abuse. Punch and Judy puppet shows, popular in England since at least the late seventeenth century, often entailed Punch beating and sometimes killing his baby, and then fighting and killing his wife and other people he came across, to the audiences' boisterous laughter. Many nursery rhymes include murder, horror and sexual abuse. One study compared violence on British television before 9 p.m., and in nursery rhymes, and came to the conclusion that the frequency of violence in nursery rhymes is around eleven times that featured in television considered safe for children.[3]

The Ancient Greek epics are catalogues of killing. The Trojan War of *The Iliad* starts off as a fight over a woman, and ends in the sack of Troy. King Agamemnon, who sacrifices his daughter for success in the war, decides that all Trojans must die, down to the babies in their mother's wombs. Odysseus is a more quick-witted character who does not have to rely on violence to get out of every problematic situation. But when he returns to Ithaca after twenty years, he kills the 108 men who had courted his wife when they thought him dead.

The Bible is also full of brutal violence – perpetrated by the good guys. In the Old Testament people casually kill, enslave and rape even family members. And the scale is staggering. When Moses discovers that some of his people worship a

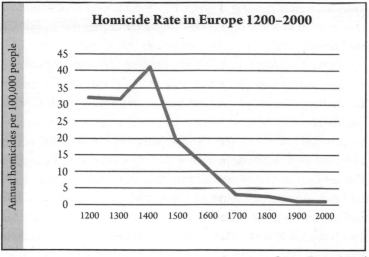

Homicide Rate in Europe 1200–2000

Source: Eisner 2003.[4]

golden calf he executes 3,000 of them, and then goes on a merciless ethnic cleansing spree, ordered by God: 'do not leave alive anything that breathes. Completely destroy them – the Hittites, Amorites, Canaanites, Perizzites, Hivites, and Jebusites – as the LORD thy God has commanded you' (Deuteronomy 20:16–17). At one point, Moses scolds his men for letting women and children survive, so he orders them to go back: 'Now kill all the boys. And kill every woman who has slept with a man, but save for yourself every girl who has never slept with a man' (Numbers 31:17–18). God even gives advice on rape himself: 'if you notice among the captives a beautiful woman and are attracted to her, you may take her as your wife' (Deuteronomy 21:11).

Today many object to the cruelty of animals in circuses, but in Roman days, the circus in 'bread and circuses' meant the killing of perhaps several million people for entertainment in arenas such as the Colosseum. Gladiators fought to the death and naked women were tied to stakes and raped or torn apart by animals. Violence was not reserved for those on the bottom rungs of Roman society: thirty-four of the forty-nine Roman Emperors who ruled before the empire was divided were murdered.

The crucifix is a symbol of Christianity, because Jesus was crucified like criminals usually were, on a cross. Saint Andrew, the patron saint of Scotland, was killed on an X-shaped cross, which is memorialized in the diagonal stripes of the Union Jack. The New Testament is more peaceful than the Old, but the medieval and early modern Christian Church found their inspiration for dealing with heretics and criminals in some of its tales about the punishments meted out in hell.

Torture and mutilation have been regularly applied in all great civilizations, from the Assyrians, Persians and Chinese to the African kingdoms and the Native American tribes, but the medieval Christian culture was more creative than most, and some of that era's best minds were occupied with coming up with ways of inflicting as much pain as possible on people before they confessed or died. As Steven Pinker summarizes it:

Torture was meted out by national and local governments throughout the Continent, and it was codified in laws that prescribed blinding, branding, amputation of hands, ears, noses and tongues, and other forms of mutilation as punishments for minor crimes. Executions were orgies of sadism, climaxing with ordeals of prolonged killing such as burning at the stake, breaking on the wheel, pulling apart by horses, impalement through the rectum, disembowelment by winding a man's intestines around a spool, and even hanging, which was a slow racking and strangulation rather than a quick breaking of the neck.[5]

We know that torture is practised today as well, especially in dictatorships, but even in some advanced democracies like the United States. But without excusing this, there are some major differences. Most often it is an exception, not a regular everyday occurrence, and the major focus is to extract information, not to inflict pain. In most cases it takes place in secrecy, hidden from view, since most people around the world now condemn it, whereas it used to be something done in the open, to the public's approval.

Medieval torture was not even a primitive and brutal way of trying to keep public violence at bay. Most of the crimes that sent people to the rack or stake were non-violent offences, sins rather than crimes that we would recognize, like heresy, blasphemy, apostasy, gossip, scolding, unconventional sexual acts and criticism of the government. The Spanish Inquisition probably killed something like 350,000 people and tortured countless others, sometimes on suspicion of having clean underwear on a Sunday or being known to take baths.

In the fifteenth century, two clergymen published the *Malleus Maleficarum*, which has been compared to a bizarre combination of Monty Python and *Mein Kampf*. It argued that witches were amongst us, and most of them were women (since women are by nature unruly, liars and so insatiable that they consort with devils). Any witches discovered had to be put to death. It was used as a handbook for the courts, and over the next two centuries, French and German witch-hunters killed between 60,000 and 100,000 women for witchcraft. The last time a British woman was executed as a witch was in 1727.

Our tales of medieval knights, written between the eleventh and thirteenth century, are of course orgies of extreme violence, often for no other reason than to prove one's bravery and honour. Knights killed for the slightest insult. Their supposed chivalry does not correspond to anything we would call by that name. One of the knight's means of battle was to ruin his enemy by killing as many of his peasants as possible, and destroying his crops and possessions. One knight tries to woo a princess by promising to rape the most beautiful women he finds in her honour.

If we want to find humanity's most violent period we have to go a long way back in time, to the traditional hunter-gatherer and hunter-horticulturalist groups. They have sometimes been romanticized as 'noble savages', but archaeological sites from 14,000 BCE to 1770 CE tell another story. We can tell the difference between a peaceful and a living death since living bones fracture like glass, with sharp, angled edges, whereas dead bones break like chalk at clean right angles. Around fifteen per cent of people in these groups faced a violent death.

But violence can also stop. One interesting example is human sacrifice, which has been practised among the Egyptians, Greeks, Romans, Scandinavians, Chinese and Japanese. Between 1440 and 1524, the Aztecs might have sacrificed forty people a day, a total of 1.2 million people. The historical explanation is a version of the problem of evil: If there is a God why is there so much evil in the world? In a world of sudden early death, violence and hunger, it was easy to assume that the gods were bloodthirsty, and if this was the case, why not try to appease them by sacrificing someone else rather than wait for them to take you?

But human sacrifice was also abolished in all cultures, often at first replaced by animal sacrifice. It could be that knowledge of history and other cultures provides evidence to counter such beliefs. It could be that greater wealth, along with longer and more predictable lives, erodes fatalism and generally leads people to value the lives of others more.

According to Steven Pinker's sources, the average annual rate of violent death for non-state societies – and this includes everything from hunter-gatherer tribes to gold rush societies in California – is 524 per 100,000. If we add all the deaths from wars, genocide, purges and man-made famines in the twentieth century, we still don't get a rate higher than 60 per 100,000 annually.[6]

The first step in the pacification process was associated with the early agricultural civilizations. They were more hierarchical and could be unbelievably brutal towards their citizens, but they did reduce the constant raiding and feuding of non-settled communities, and led to something like a five-fold decrease in rates of violent deaths.

By the thirteenth to fifteenth centuries, the homicide rate in the most advanced European regions had dropped to thirty to forty per 100,000 people per year. In London and Oxford in the fourteenth century it was as much as forty-five to 110 per 100,000. That is much lower than in non-state societies, but still thirty to forty times higher than today. For comparison, the homicide rate in the United States, which is much more violent than Europe, is now lower than five per 100,000.[7]

As Barbara Tuchman points out in her history of fourteenth-century Europe, brutal violence was a part of everyday life. On the way to church, villagers passed by criminals being flogged or chained upright in an iron collar. In church they saw images and sculptures of saints undergoing atrocious martyrdom, with arrows, spears, fire and blood everywhere, and they knew that the Church regularly used similar methods on heretics and witnesses. On their way home they might have passed by corpses, and they might have seen decapitated heads and quartered bodies impaled on stakes on the city walls. At the same time, popular entertainment meant yet more violence. Tuchman mentions villagers that bought a criminal from a neighbouring town for the pleasure of seeing him quartered by hacking him into four pieces. Other popular games included players with their hands tied behind their backs whose goal was to head-butt cats to death, or chasing pigs around a wide pen to beat them lifeless with clubs. 'It may be that the untender medieval infancy produced adults who valued others no more than they had been valued in their own formative years.'[8] It was an era filled with butchery and sadism.

But in the early modern era, something incredible happened. The European homicide rate declined from thirty to forty, to nineteen per 100,000 in the sixteenth century and eleven in the seventeenth century. In the eighteenth century it came down to 3.2 and today it is around one. In his study of historical homicide rates, Manuel Eisner explains that this process began in England and the Netherlands, the centres of modernization where urbanization, the market economy and literacy had gone the furthest. Then it spread to Scandinavia where it was higher to start with, but where it also came down faster – from forty-six per 100,000 in the fifteenth century to three in the early eighteenth century. In Italy, rates dropped dramatically only from the mid-nineteenth century.[9]

The next step in the pacification process was the institution of judicial rules and central governments. Kings put an end to the state of war between knights and turned the warlords of the Middle Ages into the courtiers of the Renaissance. Previously they had to show that they could be more brutal than the others, whereas now they had to show that they could please the king and behave in a courteous manner. The modern state built centralized administrative and judicial systems, and a system of laws and punishments that made it possible for people to maintain their social position without resorting to violence. Modern police forces, like Sir Robert Peel's 'bobbies', founded in 1828, restrained the violent on behalf of the public.

The methods of the early justice system, however, were exceptionally grim for a long time, and punishments were made public to deter others. It was not just the executions but the smaller punishments, like hands and fingers being severed, tongues ripped out, ears cut off and eyes poked out. In 1620, a traveller on his way from Dresden to Prague counted 'above seven score gallowses and wheels, where thieves were hanged, some fresh and some half rotten, and the carcasses of murderers broken limb after limb on the wheels'.[10]

If there are no centralized methods for arbitration and punishment, individuals have to be ready to defend themselves and their kin, and to build a reputation for being violent and unforgiving. 'Accidents don't happen to people who take accidents as a personal insult', as Vito Corleone puts it in *The Godfather*. This might make sense for the individual, but it also creates violent codes of honour, where men are always ready to fight back as soon as they are affronted in any way. More than a quarter of English aristocrats faced a violent death in the fourteenth and fifteenth centuries, partly because they were armed and ready to fight for their honour. The slightest insult could result in a bloody street fight between gangs of angry aristocrats.[11] Nowadays, we are familiar with such behaviour only in the cultures of organized crime, drug trafficking and other sectors where people have no recourse to law to solve their conflicts.

The classic question is: Who watches the watchers? The regent might get citizens' violence under control, but he also used violence against them, and started wars and genocides in which they died. Even though everyday violence was reduced, organized violence on a massive scale was made possible. The next step, after governments got control over people, was to give people control over the government, through the rule of law, civil liberties and democracy. Even for those in power, a peaceful way of stepping down would bring benefits. Between 600 and 1800, about one in eight European regents were murdered in office. A third of the killers took over the throne themselves.[12]

Another factor behind the reduction in crime is the rise of moral individualism, which Protestantism and the Enlightenment contributed to in different ways. Many researchers have pointed out that the downturn in violence is not always related to an increase in state centralization. But it fits with a broad cultural shift towards individual responsibility and liberation from collective bonds. People began to be seen as responsible for their crimes, and people became liberated from the obligation to avenge their kin. Combined with the rise of a state that monopolized violence, this turned settlement from being a family matter into the prerogative of judges and sovereigns. A culture of honour slowly gave way to a culture of dignity. The readiness to strike out was replaced by a readiness to control one's emotions. In Britain, the stiff upper lip became the more attractive ideal. A sharp mind and tongue were valued over a sharp sword.

A third factor was the rise of more humanitarian attitudes. As life expectancy increases and families have fewer children, the perceived value of each human life increases. Early death is no longer a norm. Many thinkers and historians have pointed out that the rise of free markets contributed to a long-term mindset and control of the emotions. Market exchange meant that other individuals became potential assets as buyers, sellers, investors or colleagues, and not just potential threats. In order to be successful on the free market, you have to understand your customer's point of view.

The Enlightenment perspective and humanist artistic movements gave insight into how others perceive loss and pain, and we now empathize more with others. Obviously there are still those who gladly inflict pain on their victims. The difference is that now even sadists and psychopaths have the right to a fair trial and must not be exposed to corporal punishment. It was a slow process, but a major turning point came in the eighteenth century. Enlightenment thinkers such as Voltaire, Montesquieu and especially Cesare Beccaria explained that criminals are human beings too and that the punishment should be proportional to the crime. The English Bill of Rights and the American Constitution banned 'cruel and unusual punishments'. Starting in countries like England and Sweden, all major European countries abolished judicial torture in the eighteenth and first half of the nineteenth century.

England abolished public hangings in 1783 and after 1834 corpses were no longer displayed on gibbets. In 1822, there were almost 300 capital offences, including forgery, shoplifting, pick pocketing, sheep theft, being in the company of gypsies for a month, and impersonating a Chelsea pensioner (in order to receive a military pension). But the use of the death penalty was on the wane and in 1861 only five capital offences remained on the books – treason, espionage, murder, piracy and arson in the royal dockyards.

During the nineteenth century, many European countries stopped carrying out the death penalty, and today all European countries except Russia and Belarus have abolished it. You couldn't guess it from the public debate, but something similar happened in the United States. From the seventeenth to the eighteenth century, the number of executions per 100,000 people per year was reduced from more than three to less than 0.5. Today it is closer to 0.1.

The government's use of violence for political purposes and for war has not diminished. In the twentieth century, the world experienced two of the bloodiest wars ever and Hitler, Mao, Stalin and other despots murdered around 120 million people. The Second World War stands out as the bloodiest war in history, with its estimated fifty-five million deaths. But despite this carnage, Steven Pinker argues that the twentieth century may not have been the bloodiest after all.

Two things cloud our judgement. First of all, we suffer from historical myopia and remember mostly what is close to us in time. If we are asked to think about violence, we think about the most recent headlines, and conclude that our time is particularly dangerous. It's more difficult for us to recall the Algerian War of Independence, which killed more than half a million people, and the Korean War where 1.2 million died, and it's even more difficult to call to mind the Thirty Years' War in which around a third of the German population perished.

The second reason why the numbers are huge today is that the world population is bigger than ever. The Mongol invasions of the thirteenth century might have killed forty million people in an era when the world population wasn't even 500 million – that's one in eight people. Adjusted for the population size at the time, it was five times worse than the Second World War. The Turco-Mongol conqueror Timur Lenk, who is infamous for constructing pyramids from the heads of thousands of the defeated, killed proportionally almost as many as Hitler, Stalin and Mao combined when he ravaged Central Asia and Persia in the fourteenth century. The fall of the Ming Dynasty in the seventeenth century was proportionally twice as big as the Second World War, and so was the fall of Rome in the third to fifth century.

One of the worst wars ever is one that almost no one has heard about, the seven-year-long An Lushan Revolt against the Chinese Tang dynasty, 756–763 CE. Estimates of the death toll vary dramatically, but the self-described atrocitologist Matthew White puts the number at thirteen million – around five per cent of the world's population in little more than seven years.[13]

Before the modern era, those wars were so much more devastating because societies were already so fragile. Without our wealth, technology and medicine, war often killed by exacerbating disease and hunger. When Napoleon retreated from Moscow in 1812, more than 400,000 of his 500,000-strong army died from pneumonia, typhus and dysentery. Germs were even deadlier than guns.

The fact that there are many more people in other places, living in peace, does not make the Second World War any less atrocious. But if we are thinking of the risk of being harmed or dying because of war, then we must also think of proportions and rates, just as we think of poverty rates and unemployment rates. In that context, no matter how counterintuitive it might sound, there is actually a case to be made that the twentieth century was the least violent century ever.

Between 900 CE and the present day, on average two new conflicts between European countries broke out every year, according to Peter Brecke's 'Conflict Catalogue'.[14] Two new wars, every year, *for 1,100 years!* Europe has been uniquely violent, but the rest of the world was not much more peaceful. Between 1400 and 1938, it lists 276 violent conflicts in the Americas, 283 in the Middle East and North Africa, 586 in sub-Saharan Africa, 313 in Central and South Asia, and 657 in East and South-East Asia. That is four new conflicts every year for a little more than 500 years, excluding Europe.[15]

Some of these wars were brutal battles for territorial conquest and some were stoked by religious fervour, but many were no more than 'pissing contests', as Pinker puts it.[16] It was a time of insecurity, so regents went to war for honour, perhaps because someone else refused to pay homage. Wars could be started because someone refused to dip a flag, salute colours or follow diplomatic procedures. Leaders genuinely believed in war; it was the natural order of things, and peace was just a brief interlude during which one rearmed and prepared for the next battle.

Just like despotism, slavery, bigotry and torture began to go out of fashion with the Enlightenment era, wars came to be seen as something to be avoided. Writers and thinkers began to attack Europe's violent history and ridiculed the idea that war confers honour. The calming of religious fundamentalism meant that countries could more often reach a negotiated conclusion. With the spread of commerce and international trade, many countries began to focus on producing value and exchanging it with neighbours, rather than stealing or destroying it. It was cheaper to buy the resources you needed than to start a war to take them. 'Where goods don't cross borders, soldiers will', as the worldview of nineteenth-century French economist Frédéric Bastiat is often summarized.

The reduction in everyday brutality also made systematic violence in wartime seem worse. As a historian of the Thirty Years' War in the seventeenth century has pointed out, war did not seem as awful to people who were already used to violence in their lives:

> Bloodshed, rape, robbery, torture, and famine were less revolting to a people whose ordinary life was encompassed by them in milder forms. Robbery with violence was common enough in peace-time, torture was inflicted at most criminal trials, horrible and prolonged executions were performed before great audiences; plague and famine effected their repeated and indiscriminate devastations.[17]

The change in attitude could be seen in leaders' rhetoric. Where they used to say that war would bring them glory, now they had to start claiming that they really, really wanted peace and had been forced into war by a belligerent enemy. As the scholar of international relations John Mueller notes: 'No longer was it possible simply and honestly to proclaim like Julius Caesar, "I came, I saw, I conquered." Gradually this was changed to "I came, I saw, he attacked me while I was just standing there looking, I won".'[18]

A fascinating example of changing attitudes to war and peace is Sweden. It used to be one of the great European powers, and the Baltic Sea used to be a Swedish inland sea. In 1809, Sweden lost its eastern half – Finland – to Russia, and even chose one of Napoleon's Marshals as the new king, with the hope that he would restore past glories. But as time went by, and an opportunity for modest affluence began to spread, the Swedish élite lost their interest in military adventures. One of the most influential writers, Esaias Tegnér wrote an epic poem that concluded that if Swedes worked hard and created more prosperity we could 're-conquer Finland within Sweden's borders'. This became a mantra for many Swedish nineteenth-century politicians who thought that a new Swedish empire could only be built with education, railways, economic reform and free trade. As eager as previous Swedish leaders had been to pick a fight with Russia, Denmark or Poland, this generation of politicians did everything they could to keep Sweden out of war. In Denmark, the Netherlands, Spain and Portugal, the story was similar. When they lost wars they no longer looked for revenge. Instead they turned their backs on the battlefields. They started making money – not war.

One of Steven Pinker's ways of looking at the frequency of warfare in history is to look at the 'Great Powers', including Britain and France, Russia after 1721, Prussia/Germany after 1740, the USA after 1898, China after 1949, Japan 1905–45, Italy 1861–1943, the Netherlands and Sweden before the late eighteenth century, the Ottoman Empire until 1699, Spain until 1808, and all entities under the Habsburg dynasty until 1918.

In the sixteenth and seventeenth centuries, the Great Powers were at war seventy-five to 100% of the years. Since then the trend points steadily downwards, especially after the Napoleonic Wars in the early nineteenth century. The quarter-century from 1950 to 1975 had only one war between the great powers – US and China in the Korean War. Since then, there has not been one. The number of wars involving a Great Power has also declined and so has their duration. Such a war used to last on average four to ten years. The four wars involving great powers in the last quarter of the twentieth century lasted on average ninety-seven days. However, modern technology and military organization made those wars more lethal until the mid-twentieth century.[19]

The First and Second World Wars were dramatic reversals of a several hundred year-long decline in conflicts. But they also gave impetus to a peace movement that was stronger than ever. After the carnage, people everywhere concluded that war was immoral and uncivilized. Photographers, writers and artists tried to show people the repulsive reality of war. It does something to your attitude to war when you see a picture of a nine-year-old girl, running for her life from a napalm attack, on the cover of your morning newspaper. It makes it more difficult to talk about glory, or of how the enemy got what they deserved.

The United Nations was founded in 1945, with the explicit goal of avoiding another such conflict, and it worked hard to make borders sacrosanct. The old idea that war was merely the continuation of politics by other means, just one of the tools for statecraft, was replaced by the idea that war is a crime and illegal unless in self-defence. European powers gave up the idea of territorial expansion and dismantled their empires, sometimes after revolts and conflict, sometimes peacefully, which meant the end of colonial wars and atrocities. A new Cold War between America and its allies and the Soviet Union broke out, and many experts were certain that it had to end in a global war at some point, with the possibility of global nuclear annihilation. It didn't. It resulted in proxy wars and civil strife in several countries, but World War III never came.

On 15 May 1984, the world's major powers had managed to remain at peace with one another for the longest stretch of time since the days of the Roman Empire, according to John Mueller. With the exception of the Soviet invasion of Hungary in 1956, there had been no wars between the forty-four richest countries in the world during that time. 'Never before in history have so many well-armed, important countries spent so much time not using their arms against each other.'[20]

Mueller explains that war had been the result of governments thinking that war was inevitable and that they might gain from it if they struck at the right time, in the right way. Now countries know it can be avoided and most believe that they would lose from it. Some think that the threat of nuclear war has kept the Great Powers from fighting, but if that were the only reason, the world would have become much less secure after the Cold War. In fact, the opposite has happened. In the 1980s, there were on average forty-three state-based armed conflicts every year, with a peak of fifty-two in 1991 and 1992. Then this began to decline to around thirty in the early 2000s, before climbing back to forty now.

These numbers hide the most important shift, that those conflicts have become much less lethal, perhaps because the world is watching, and one can lose the public relations war even as one physically gains ground. The average interstate war killed 86,000 people in the 1950s and 39,000 in the 1970s. Today, it kills slightly more than 3,000 people. Civil wars today kill less than a third of the numbers they did in the 1960s to 1980s. This is partly the result of a new international security architecture, which focuses on conflict prevention when there is a risk of war and peace-making when there is one.[21]

This may come as a surprise since we often read that the number of civilian victims is increasing. It is often repeated, by UN institutions and others, that 100 years ago ten per cent of the deaths in war were suffered by civilians, whereas today it is ninety per cent. After an investigation of the number, the Human Security Report concluded that 'it has no basis in fact'. It seems to have originated in calculation errors, guesses without sources and the confusion of fatalities and refugees. It is very difficult to find data, but the report suggests a span between thirty and sixty per cent of fatalities, and there is no evidence that this has increased over the years.[22] On the contrary, civilian deaths used to be something considered unavoidable or even necessary to scare the enemy. Now many governments, especially democratic governments under the public's watchful eye, do what they can to avoid it. Around 5,300 civilians died in Afghanistan from 2004 to 2010 (mostly killed by the Taliban). In the Vietnam War, at least 800,000 civilians were killed.

Something similar seems to have happened with genocide. It is not that it has stopped altogether, but it is now universally condemned to the extent that all United Nations members have committed to stopping it when it takes place. It used to be so common that historians didn't care much about it. In a history of genocide starting from the Athenian destruction of Melos and the Roman massacre of the Carthaginians, Frank Chalk and Kurt Jonassohn write that genocide 'has been practiced in all regions of the world and during all periods in history'. But you couldn't always guess it from what the historians wrote at the time:

> We know that empires disappeared and that cities were destroyed, and we suspect that some wars were genocidal in their results; but we do not know what happened to the bulk of the populations involved in these events. Their fate was simply too unimportant. When they were mentioned at all, they were

usually lumped together with the herds of oxen, sheep, and other livestock.[23]

It was only after the unrivalled evil of the Holocaust that the victims began to tell their own story, and advocates of Nazism felt the need to deny that it had ever happened. It was a unique episode of industrial destruction of an entire people, which changed the world's perspective of genocide. Even during the war, when Americans were asked what should be done with the Japanese after a decisive victory, ten to fifteen per cent volunteered the response that they should be exterminated.

After the fall of the various forms of fascism and communism there have been some genocides, as in Bosnia in 1992–5 and Rwanda in 1994, but these are spikes in a downward trend. The beginning of the twenty-first century has been more free from genocide than any other period of the last hundred years. Average annual death tolls from one-sided violence have halved since the 1990s, even excluding the genocide in Rwanda.[24]

One form of one-sided violence that has increased, on the other hand, is terrorism, especially terrorist attacks perpetrated in the name of religion. The number of people who have died from terrorist activity has increased five-fold since 2000, according to the Global Terrorism Index. This is the result of a terrorist surge in Iraq, Syria, Afghanistan, Pakistan and Nigeria, often in situations resembling war zones. We have also seen an increase in attacks in western Europe in the last few years, even though the death toll is still only around two-thirds of what it was in the 1970s, when both separatist and communist terror groups were active.

Terrorism is spectacular, dramatic and frightening. Indeed, that is the whole point of terrorism: to sow fear. But it kills very few. It is not on the scale of other acts of violence like war or criminality, and it is not even close to traffic deaths. Since 2000, around 400 people have died from terrorism in the OECD countries every year, mostly in Turkey and Israel. More Europeans drown in their own bathtubs, and ten times more die falling down the stairs.[25]

Contrary to popular belief, terror is a very inefficient way of accomplishing ideological goals. For a long time, it was considered efficient because of the success of violent anti-colonial campaigns, but opposition to colonialism succeeded whether it was violent or not. Violent campaigns in general are great failures. The political scientist Audrey Cronin looked at 457 terrorist groups active since 1968. None of them managed to conquer a state and ninety-four per cent of them failed to secure even one of their operative goals. The typical terrorist organization survived only for eight years, partly because the attacks on civilians alienated the population that the group wanted support from: 'terrorist violence contains within itself the seeds of repulsion and revulsion. Violence has an international language, but so does decency.'[26]

So it seems that the only way for terrorists to win is if its victims overreact, dismantle civil liberties and blame whole groups for the actions of a few. Doing so stirs up the very conflicts that the terrorists seek and makes it easier to recruit terrorists and continue the battle.

Peace is never a certainty. When we feel threatened, our fight or flight instinct is activated, and it is tempting to reach for weapons. In his 1909 book *The Great Illusion*, the English social democrat Norman Angell made an excellent case that industrialized states would no longer benefit from conquest, partly because of the close economic interconnection between countries.[27] Five years later the First World War broke out, between countries that did not just trade with one another, but whose monarchs – King George V, Kaiser Wilhelm II and Tsar Nicholas II – were cousins and used to socialize.

Many experts fear that a major war could result from a rising China trying to battle the United States for naval supremacy in East Asia, or from a revanchist Russia trying to regain lost ground in Europe. Conflicts in the Middle East might result in a war between big powers, and India and Pakistan are two nuclear states that often threaten each other with war. The élite in rogue states like North Korea might prefer to unleash hell rather than go quietly. Not least, nuclear proliferation means that the world is always at risk. We know that there are well-funded terrorist groups working hard to kill as many civilians as possible. And at some point a terrorist group might lay their hands on a nuclear device.

But the overall trends are strong. Increasing wealth and health and smaller families seem to have made us value life more, and this has resulted in more humanitarian attitudes and a stronger interest in peace. Commerce and trade has made countries more interested in mutually beneficial exchange than in zero-sum games. To this we may add an entirely new phenomenon among affluent liberal democracies: something we might call a true peace. Their people and leaders can't even dream of going to war against each other again, even traditional arch enemies like France and Germany.

It seems that democracies very rarely go to war against each other, perhaps because voters rarely want war, leaders rarely gain politically from it, and perhaps also because democracy's rule-based domestic negotiations have been externalized. The political scientists Bruce Russett and John Oneal have documented that this democratic peace theory is very strong, at least after the year 1900. Great powers are more war-prone than others, even though they are democratic, but two democracies almost never fight each other. Russett and Oneal expand on this thesis and argue that it may not be a democratic peace, after all, but a liberal peace, since free trade and economic interdependence have a greater effect than democracy. There is a democratic peace only when both countries are democratic, whereas the effects of trade and commerce can be seen even when only one of the countries has an open market economy. As the Austrian economist Ludwig von Mises put it, if the tailor goes to war against the baker, he must henceforth bake his own bread.[28]

There are disputes between liberal democracies as well, of course, but the difference is how they are resolved. Hans Island, a small, uninhabited island in the Kennedy Channel between Canada's Ellesmere Island and northern Greenland, is claimed by both Canada and Denmark. The countries' militaries do visit the island once in a while. When the Danish military visits the island, they leave a bottle of Danish schnapps. When the Canadian military visit they leave a bottle of Canadian Club and a sign saying, 'Welcome to Canada.'

6

THE ENVIRONMENT

Are not poverty and need the greatest polluters? . . . How can
we speak to those who live in villages and in slums about keeping the oceans, the rivers and the air clean when their own lives
are contaminated at the source? The environment cannot be
improved in conditions of poverty.

Indira Gandhi[1]

On Friday, 5 December 1952, the undertaker Stan Cribb and
his uncle led a line of cars full of mourners through the streets
of London to a wake, when they noticed something ominous
in front of them. 'You had this swirling, like somebody had set
a load of car tires on fire.' The gathering fog grew darker and
after a few minutes, Cribb couldn't even see the kerb. His uncle
got out and walked in front of the hearse with a powerful hurri-
cane lantern, to lead the hearse forward. But it was useless. 'It's
like you were blind,' says Cribb.[2]

A Great Smog had settled over London, and it would stay
there for four horrible days. The cold had made Londoners
burn more coal, and the smoke, combined with pollutants
from industrial processes, from vehicles and from across the
English Channel, formed a thick layer over the city. Cars were

abandoned and people had to feel their way home along railings. A nurse explained that the smog penetrated clothes and blackened undergarments.

Cribb and his uncle would have a lot of work in the weeks to come. Smog contains soot particulates and sulphur dioxide, which is poisonous. Hundreds of people died immediately, and mortality sharply increased for several months. One study estimates that as many as 12,000 people might have been killed by the Great Smog.[3]

This was the most lethal instance of smog, but London often suffered from it by varying degrees, just like many big cities in developing countries do today. From the Victorian era onwards, it was nicknamed a 'pea souper' because the tarry particles of soot turned the air yellow-black. It was so frequent that it formed the natural landscape for much of the literature of the time. Smog is part of Sherlock Holmes's London, where mud-coloured clouds hang over the muddy streets. In Charles Dickens's *Bleak House* Esther thinks there is a fire somewhere when she arrives in London because the streets are so filled with dense smoke that scarcely anything can be seen.

The affluence and the development that saved humanity from poverty and early death exacted a brutal price on our environment. Increased production and transportation reduced poverty, but also resulted in emissions that damaged the air, rivers, lakes and lungs. The expansion of farming and the use of artificial fertilizer reduced hunger, but resulted in oxygen depletion and dead zones in many lakes. The burning of fossil fuels, which powered humanity's industrial ascent, also warmed the climate, with a number of detrimental consequences possible during the twenty-first century. As long as human life remained nasty, brutish and short, we did not have the will, nor the ability, to deal with these problems effectively.

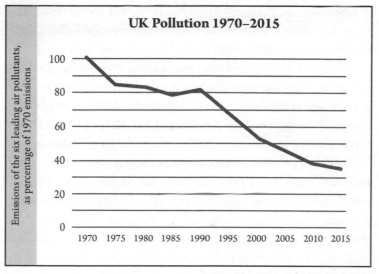

Source: Department for Environment,
Food and Rural Affairs 2014.[4]

In the decades after the Second World War, with the advent of peace and the first signs of global prosperity, attention began to be drawn to the environment. A green movement picked up speed in the West, led by intellectuals and activists. Many looked at environmental trends and feared that if they were to continue, we would soon see a future with an overcrowded planet, where humanity used up all its natural resources, from oil to metals and minerals. People imagined a world without forests, with acid rain, where people had to wear surgical masks to protect themselves from emissions, where most species were extinct and humanity suffered from an explosion in cancer because of all the chemicals being used in nature. Wealth and technology were not compatible with a green, breathing planet.

There are still huge environmental problems, but if you look at the developed world today, it looks nothing like the scenarios envisioned in the 1960s and 1970s. Some of our ideas were dramatically wrong and not backed up by science, but the world we live in now is also the result of a concerted effort to avoid those scenarios.

In 1972, the enormously influential Club of Rome warned: 'Virtually every pollutant that has been measured as a function of time appears to be increasing exponentially.'[5] But soon pollution didn't just stop increasing, it began to decrease – dramatically. According to the United States Environmental Protection Agency, total emissions of six leading air pollutants were reduced by more than two-thirds from 1980 to 2014. Volatile organic compounds were reduced by fifty-three per cent, nitrogen dioxide by fifty-five per cent, direct particulate matter by fifty-eight per cent, carbon monoxide by sixty-nine per cent, sulphur dioxide by eighty-one per cent and lead by ninety-nine per cent.[6]

In Britain, the emission of volatile organic compounds fell by sixty per cent, nitrogen oxides by sixty-two per cent, particulate matter by an average of seventy-seven per cent and sulphur dioxide by ninety-four per cent from 1970 to 2013.[7] According to a long-term data series, the concentration of smoke and sulphur dioxide in London air from the late sixteenth century increased for 300 years, but then dropped off almost overnight. As statistician Bjørn Lomborg summarizes it, 'the London air has not been cleaner than today since the Middle Ages.'[8]

In the 1980s the international community realized that a huge hole in the ozone layer over Antarctica was expanding and could expose life on earth to damaging ultraviolet light. By international agreement in Montreal, countries phased out the substances that eroded the ozone layer. This worked exceptionally well and the layer is now slowly recovering, possibly saving humanity from hundreds of millions of cases of skin cancer.

The Thames is an example of how rivers and lakes have returned to health after industrial pollution has decreased and sewage companies have been forced to treat water and maintain adequate collecting systems. In 1957, the filthy and stinking river was declared biologically dead. Today, it is in excellent health with 125 different species of fish. In 2008, the short-snouted seahorse, which is extremely sensitive to pollution, was back in the Thames.[9]

The number of oil spills in our oceans has also been reduced dramatically. In the 1970s, there was an average of twenty-four oil spills per year. Since 2000, there has been an average of less than three. In the years 2000 to 2014, a total amount of 234,000 tonnes were spilt. This may sound like a lot, but is much less than the *annual* amount spilt in the 1970s. The quantity of oil spilt has been reduced by ninety-nine per cent between 1970 and 2014.[10]

After warnings of dying forests in eastern Europe in the late 1970s and the 1980s, many feared that acid rain would turn Europe's forests into chemical deserts. But it never happened, partly because pollution levels fell, partly because the alarms were exaggerated. In the EU, the ecosystem area where acidification critical loads are exceeded declined from forty-three to seven per cent from 1980 to 2010, and eutrophication (such as algal blooms in rivers and lakes) is also on the decline.[11]

Deforestation has stopped in wealthy countries. Europe's forest area grew by more than 0.3% annually from 1990 to 2015. In United States it is growing by 0.1% annually. The global annual rate of forest loss has slowed from 0.18 to 0.008%

since the early 1990s. In fact, the forests are also coming back in many developing countries. In China, the forest cover is now growing by more than two million hectares per year. In the Brazilian Amazon, for a long time almost synonymous with deforestation, the annual rate has declined by seventy per cent since 2005, thanks to better forest protection and farmers boosting yields on existing farmland.[12]

As we saw in the chapter on food, farming technologies employed since the early 1960s have saved an area equal to two South Americas from being turned into farmland. Between 1995 and 2010, land used for farming increased only by 0.04% annually. The researchers Jesse Ausubel and Iddo Wernick even project that humanity has reached 'peak farmland', and that land use for agriculture will decline by 0.2% annually from 2010 to 2060. They say that they 'believe humanity now stands at Peak Farmland, and the 21st century will see the release of vast areas of land, hundreds of millions of hectares, more than twice the area of France for nature'.[13] Urbanization has also helped, since city dwellers use less energy and less water and produce less pollution than people in rural areas, but they also use less land.

This has saved us from some of the most horrible extinction scenarios. Humanity has always threatened wildlife and other species, and we do that now as well. As tropical rainforests are cut down, species-rich environments are being depleted, and overfishing has caused many fish stocks to suffer and some to collapse. In 1975 Paul and Anne Ehrlich predicted that around half of all species on the planet would have become extinct by now. Since the world is estimated to be home to something like five to fifteen million species, several million would have gone extinct since then. But the International Union for the

Conservation of Nature lists no more than 709 species as having become extinct since 1500.[14] Most of these extinctions have taken place in isolated areas, such as oceanic islands, which suggests that many life forms are flexible and can migrate and survive in modified environments.

We must remember that recorded cases are not the same as the number that have really become extinct, since we haven't discovered all species. But it's surprisingly difficult to find hard proof of a mass extinction. One interesting study published in *Science* looked at 100 biodiversity time series in marine and terrestrial habitats from the last 150 years, expecting to find 'that most assemblages would exhibit a decrease in local diversity through time'. They were surprised to find the distribution of diversity slopes centred around zero, with the majority being statistically very close to zero. That is to say, the composition of species changed, but they found 'no evidence for a consistent or even an average negative trend'.[15]

There are known unknowns – many species that we don't even have a name for are becoming extinct. But we also know for certain that without urbanization, the protection of forests and more efficient agriculture, things would be much worse. And many of the most interesting areas with the most biological diversity are now being protected at pace. Protected areas nearly doubled from 8.5% to 14.3% of the world's total land area between 1990 and 2013. An area twice the size of the United States is now protected.

Today, it seems like technology and affluence are not an obstacle to environmental sustainability, but rather its precondition. The world's most polluted places are not London, New York and Paris, but cities like Beijing and New Delhi. The Environmental Performance Index is an attempt to measure environmental sustainability around the world, focusing on nine issue areas comprised of twenty indicators.[16] 'Wealth emerges as a major determinant of environmental performance' was one of its first conclusions. The wealthier the country, the more it had done to clean up the environment and to make it safe for humanity. Countries such as Australia, Germany, Sweden and Britain come out on top, whereas we find countries such as Haiti, Sudan, Liberia and Somalia at the bottom.[17]

What happened? Why has the predicted eco-disaster not yet taken place? First of all, preferences changed with better living conditions. If you are being asked to choose between the long-term prospect of the forest or river close by, or the immediate survival and well-being of your children, there really is no choice. But as wealth grew, children survived and parents could afford to invest in their future, the question became whether they would like to have a little more money in their wallet or a sustainable forest or river. Given a decent quality of life, many chose the latter. The growth of the environmental movement since the 1970s is in itself a result of these changing perspectives. The attention given to the risks gave us the impetus to do something about it, in our roles as consumers and as voters. The Great Smog of 1952 drove British politicians to pass a Clean Air Act in 1956, which introduced smoke control areas and precipitated a shift from dirty coal to cleaner coals, electricity and gas.

At the same time, technological progress created new opportunities to produce and transport in a more environmentally friendly way. Waste water treatment and solid-waste management also reduced our damage to the environment. The use of filters, scrubbers, adsorbers and smarter processes reduced emissions from factories. Cars became cleaner. Amazingly, a modern car in motion emits less pollution than a 1970s car did in the parking lot, turned off, due to gasoline vapour leakage.[18]

Similarly, the much feared and publicized cancer epidemic has never appeared. The fact that we get cancer more often today is down to the fact that we get older. As the US National Cancer Institute points out, it is really a good sign: 'This only appears to be the case because the number of new cancer cases reported is rising as the population is both expanding and ageing.'[19] The median age of a cancer diagnosis is sixty-five years. In 1900, life expectancy in the richest countries was around fifty years. More people get cancer now because people in previous eras did not survive long enough to get cancer.

And in almost every age group, the incidence rate is falling. Institutions like the WHO estimate that pollution and chemicals in our environment account for no more than three per cent of all cancers, and most of those cases are people in industries that are exposed to high levels of chemicals on the job. The National Academy of the Sciences concludes that the synthetic components of our diet might even be safer than the natural components.[20] The idea that natural is good and artificial is bad has no basis in science. Tobacco, after all, is natural.

We constantly underestimate our own creativity. The fear that we would exhaust the planet's resources rested on a simple and intuitive model where we use a certain quantity of raw materials (for example, coal) to get what we want (for example, energy). We have a fixed quantity of coal, we need a constant proportion of coal to get the energy we use, and as the population grows we use more and more energy. Coal, consequently, will run out. This was the model popularized by the Club of Rome.

The economist Julian Simon asserted that this theory is wrong on almost every point. Yes, there is a certain quantity of a certain given resource, he pointed out, but the quantities are not limited in the way we believe they are. There are reserves we have yet to discover, reserves which are not yet economically viable, and the possibility of recycling. We do not use resources in constant proportions – on the contrary, we are using ever smaller quantities of resources per unit of output. Moreover, demand is not for the resource in itself but for what we do or make with it, and new technology and ingenuity will enable us to find other, hitherto unforeseen resources to achieve our needs. If the market is relatively free, a shortage will mean higher prices, in which case we will economize more with that raw material, and should a resource run out, we will find or invent substitutes. The most important resource is the human brain, a resource which is pleasantly reproducible.

Julian Simon was proven right. Stocks of almost all the resources which the Club of Rome was worried about have increased. Several have quadrupled. In 1972, the Club's computer models said that known copper reserves would run out in thirty-six years, especially if the Chinese got telephone connections. Since this was more than forty years ago, copper should be gone by now. Back then, it was estimated that there would be accessible reserves of about 280 million metric tons of copper. Since then almost 480 million metric tons have been consumed – more than the original reserves – and world copper reserves are now estimated to be more than double, at 700 million metric tons of copper. If we include probable deposits, we probably have 100 to 200 years of copper supplies left.[21]

The resources have been used in a more efficient way, new deposits have been discovered and new technology has made it possible to extract deposits that were previously inaccessible. In addition, we have reduced our dependence on copper, because it has been replaced by better material. Telephone connections now use fibre optic cables, not copper wire, and increasingly wireless technology.

So we never ran out of resources. They did not even increase in price. The real price of raw materials, as reflected by the *Economist*'s industrial commodity price-index sunk by roughly half from 1871 to 2010, even though that was before the commodity price cycle ran out of steam. This translates into an annual compound growth of –0.5% per year for almost 140 years.[22]

The fact that rich countries are solving many environmental problems shows that humanity is finding ways of dealing even with these. But at the same time, the situation in many poor and middle-income countries is bad, and getting worse, as agriculture, industry and transportation grow rapidly. And the number of people breathing unsafe air has risen by more than 600 million since 2000, to a total of almost 1.8 billion.[23] Many cities in India, Pakistan and Bangladesh suffer from pollution levels that are ten times higher than what is deemed safe. Levels of fine particulate matter in the air are around six times higher in China than in countries like Sweden, Britain and the United States. Smog is now a regular occurrence in fast-growing Chinese cities.

It is important to realize that this process of industrialization and wealth creation in poor countries is a way of dealing with even more acute and dangerous problems, just like the Industrial Revolution in the West increased pollution, but solved the urgent problems of early death and poverty. It is not just that this process helps to reduce poverty and mortality generally; it also helps deal with traditional environmental problems that pose a more immediate risk to human life.

The worst environmental problems in poor countries stem not from technology and affluence, but from the lack of technology and affluence. For lack of electricity, gas and paraffin, billions of people have to cook by burning wood, dung, charcoal and coal in open fires or simple stoves. In one third of all countries, more than half the population use solid fuels, especially in Africa and South Asia. This is done indoors, because outside it is too hot in the dry season and too wet in the rainy season, and it is too difficult to retain the heat in one place with a wind blowing. This results in pulmonary disease and lung cancer and, in children, pneumonia and other acute lower respiratory diseases. According to the Global Burden of Disease project, household air pollution claims the lives of 3.5 million people annually. If this is accurate, bad indoor air kills one person every ten seconds.

As we have seen before, lack of access to safe water and sanitation might be even more lethal. These are the kinds of traditional environmental threats that have been solved in industrialized countries, and we shouldn't think it strange that poor countries welcome industrial production and modern energy sources, even if that creates new environmental problems.

The hope is that the changes in preferences and technology that have begun to turn the situation around in the West will also hold true for poor countries as they grow richer. There are some signs that the rest of the world is beginning to control water and air pollution. Out of the 178 countries in the Environmental Performance Index, 172 countries actually registered an improvement in performance between 2004 and 2014. A mere six countries performed worse.

Interestingly, poor countries often begin to clean up their act at a much earlier stage of development than rich countries did. This is partly because they can learn from our mistakes, but also because green technologies that were developed in industrialized countries can be used straight away in poorer countries. One example is unleaded gasoline. The United States started using it in 1975. India and China made the same transition in 1997, at which point they had only thirteen per cent of the wealth of Americans in 1975.[24]

In the literature, the possibility of an environmental 'Kuznets curve' (EKC) is often discussed. According to this, many forms of environmental degradation follow an inverted U-curve. As countries start to get richer, the damage to the environment grows, but after a certain point further income growth results in improvements. A recent review of 878 observations from 103 empirical studies between 1992 and 2009 concluded that there are several such income turning points: 'Results indicate the presence of an EKC-type relationship for landscape degradation, water pollution, agricultural wastes, municipal-related wastes and several air pollution measures.'[25]

This gives us hope for many poor countries that are rapidly approaching such incomes. However, there is one important exception: the emissions of carbon dioxide from fossil fuels, which does not begin to decline until very high income levels are attained. This is worrying, since more CO^2 and other so-called greenhouse gases in the atmosphere make the global climate warmer and more unstable than would otherwise be the case.

What this will result in is hotly debated. There is a broad spectrum of possible outcomes, from minor and even beneficial changes all the way to global disaster, and a lot of it depends on how much temperatures will rise. More CO^2 increases global biomass production, and despite what we hear during every heat wave, more people die because of cold weather than warm. Almost twice as many Americans died from excess cold than from excess heat from 1979 to 2006.[26]

But if the temperature increases too much it might lead to floods, droughts, eradication of species, tropical diseases, hurricanes and melting glaciers all becoming more frequent. The consequences and the costs may be very large, especially in poor countries, which do not have the resources and technology necessary to handle rapid adjustments. Even if a worst-case scenario might be unlikely, it is worth insuring ourselves against it by limiting climate change. You don't have to think that the house will burn down to buy insurance against it.

But drastic and far-reaching efforts to limit carbon dioxide emissions might be counter-productive. It is not necessarily true that the best way forward is to limit emissions to such an extent as to prevent climate change. What is important is that our climate policies don't hurt our ability to create more wealth and better technologies and to bring power to the world's poor. That would be a case of killing the patient to cure the disease. The biggest problems in the world are still problems of poverty and traditional environmental hazards, such as polluted air and water. Forcing too many restraints and costs on today's global population might make life more difficult for the poor today because we want to reduce the risks to tomorrow's rich.

It's easy to say that poor countries should just use solar power or other forms of renewable sources rather than fossil fuels, but with the state of today's technology, it is often too costly, and does not give sufficiently reliable power. Ten billion dollars invested in burning gas to power a population could help lift ninety million people out of poverty. If the same amount was spent only on renewables, it would only help twenty to twenty-seven million people, leaving more than sixty million in poverty and darkness and thousands to suffer an early death.[27]

We also need greater wealth and technological development in any case, to meet new problems, from the global warming that will happen whatever we do now, and from other kinds of threats, such as recurrent pandemics, earthquakes, tsunamis, super-volcanic eruptions, meteorite impacts or natural climate change. Banking everything on countering one single risk will make us more vulnerable to other problems, even if that particular risk, according to present-day computer models, is the worst one of all.

The worst damage always occurs in poor countries, in part as a direct result of their poverty. We often measure the size of a disaster by its financial cost, but rich countries can suffer larger financial losses because they have greater assets to begin with; this says nothing about the actual extent of damage. According to UN data, ninety-five per cent of all deaths from natural disasters between 1970 and 2008 occurred in poor and middle-income countries. With greater wealth we also get safer construction, building codes, health care, effective warning systems and better preventive work. As the author and science correspondent Ronald Bailey puts it: 'Bad weather produces death and destruction largely when it encounters poverty.'[28]

There is a popular perception that technology-dependent civilizations are worse at handling a collapse than others, because they are so dependent on complex systems that might fail. It seems intuitive and plays into the collapse anxiety that rich Westerners, dependent on technologies we don't understand, often feel. But it does not seem to be correct. When relatively developed Yugoslavia imploded during the wars of the early 1990s, people there were able to apply innovative solutions to maintain at least a minimum level of hygiene, safe water, and energy for heating and cooking. When civil war broke out in already underdeveloped Sierra Leone, no such improvised safety net could be created and its population fell into destitution of prehistoric proportions. A textbook on global health summarizes it neatly: 'Quite contrary to common perceptions, highly-developed, technological societies seem to have better resources to maintain health during a war than poorer societies using less modern technology.'[29]

If this is the case, natural disasters should become less destructive over time, as the world gets richer, and that is indeed what the data suggest. Even though the population at risk is growing constantly, since population is growing and we build in more dangerous places, such as coastal areas, the number of casualties is declining. One paper looked at all deaths from the 8,498 droughts, wildfires, storms, floods, wet mass movement (like avalanches and landslides) and extreme temperature events reported between 1900 and 2008 in the EM-DAT's International Disaster Database. Since the 1920s the number of deaths from these weather events has declined almost every decade, even though population grew dramatically. Annual mortality for these events declined by eighty-four per cent between the 1900–89 and 1990–2008 periods. The annual mortality rate – the risk of dying from a natural disaster – declined by an astonishing ninety-four per cent.[30]

This is important, since all the experience and every model suggest that the largest damage from global warming will happen in poor countries. They need development to counter it. If annual global economic growth remains around two per cent per head, the average person in 100 years' time will be around eight times richer than today's average person. With those resources, the level of scientific knowledge, and the technological solutions that may then be at our disposal, many of the problems that intimidate us today will be much easier to handle – from adapting to warming to taking CO^2 out of the atmosphere.

There are ways of reducing carbon dioxide without reducing growth, trade and access to energy. These include more efficient production processes, less energy-consuming construction and new energy sources and fuels. Recently, I made a documentary on the world economy where I took a close look at the impressive and brand new container ship *Mærsk Mc-Kinney Møller*. It is an ocean-going behemoth over twenty storeys high and 1,300 feet long. If the ship's 18,000 containers were loaded aboard a train, the carriages would be sixty-eight miles long. But despite its unnatural size, it is probably the most environmentally friendly way of transporting goods yet invented.

This is partly just because it is built to carry so many containers, but also because of a state of the art propulsion system, an ultra-long stroke engine designed to squeeze as many miles as possible out of every drop of oil. It revolves at a slower pace than usual, but compensates for it with a larger propeller diameter.

Innovations like these make it possible to do more with less. The amount of energy required to produce a unit of wealth has declined by around one per cent per year in the past 150 years in the Western world, and that pace has accelerated. If technology in the United States had been frozen at the 1900 level, Americans would be emitting three times more CO^2 than they do today.

The fact that our efficiency is improving is not enough to reduce emissions, since tomorrow, there will be more people on the planet, and they will all produce more than they did yesterday. CO_2 emissions do not follow the economy's growth in a linear way any more, but they are still growing.

In some advanced countries, however, the turning point might already have been reached. The United States, Britain and the European Union have reduced total CO_2 emissions since 2000. If green technology is helping us to reduce emissions and richer countries are making more use of them, it seems that wealth and technology are not necessarily the problem even when it comes to carbon dioxide. It indicates that the solution is not to turn around and go back, but to intensify existing trends, ensuring that alternative fuels and forms of energy are developed and become cheaper. Putting a price on emissions, with a revenue-neutral carbon tax, so that people pay for the CO_2 they emit, would help.

Scientists and entrepreneurs are hard at work trying to improve on old technologies, inventing new ones and finding completely new roads ahead. Generation III nuclear reactors have better thermal efficiency, superior fuel technology and passive safety systems that rely on physical phenomena to cool down in the event of an emergency. This has improved safety, reduced cost and extended their operational life by about a third. The Fukushima Daiichi disaster was the result of a power-loss that made it impossible to cool the radioactive and spent fuel. A passive safety system would have used nothing but gravity to circulate water to cool down the plant, and would also have circulated cool outside air.

Right now scientists and companies are working on Generation IV nuclear power. It is a summary term for reactors that are so far only experimental. They all have passive safety systems, get hundreds of times more energy from the same fuel and don't have the same problems with waste. Fast reactors can burn the waste as well. One clever safety innovation is that a fast reactor burns liquid metal fuels. When they overheat, the fuels expand and slow down the reaction on their own. A Chernobyl or Harrisburg disaster would not be possible.

The real game changer would be the small, modular reactors that some companies are working on. Bill Gates has invested in TerraPower, which wants to build a travelling wave reactor that uses radioactive waste as a fuel, doesn't have to be refuelled and cannot melt down. The idea is to have them built in factories, completely sealed and set to run for several decades without human intervention. The reactor could also serve as its own burial casket. If this works, they could just be dropped into a concrete hole – 'build, bury, and forget'. TerraPower's founder thinks that we could 'power the world for the next one thousand years just burning and disposing of the depleted uranium and spent fuel rods in today's stockpiles'.[31]

Ethanol in the versions governments have subsidized was a costly failure, but now we are starting to see exciting developments in bio-fuels. Both big oil companies and small, innovative startups are working on a new generation of biofuels made from algae. They can produce thirty times more energy per acre than traditional ethanol, and the goal is to modify them to produce hundreds of times more energy. That is not the only advantage; they can also be grown anywhere, so they don't have to compete with valuable farmland, and they can use seawater instead of freshwater. Since algae feed on CO_2, we could turn the smokestacks around and feed them our emissions.

There are also fascinating new possibilities that might help us get more energy from the sun. Graphene is an incredible new material created in 2004 at the University of Manchester. It is unbelievably thin and flexible, just one carbon atom thick, which makes it almost two-dimensional. At the same time it is remarkably strong, doesn't corrode and conducts heat and electricity efficiently. This one material could drastically change the economics of solar power, because most solar cells today use expensive indium, whereas carbon atoms are not exactly rare. So far graphene is not very good at collecting the electrical current from the solar cells, but scientists are hard at work trying to solve that problem. If they do, we could turn anything into a solar power station in the future. Imagine if your house, your clothes, your car or the road was covered in solar film.

This isn't even the most exciting of the technologies we are working on. In laboratories around the world, tens of thousands of scientists and engineers are trying to revolutionize energy – from making our everyday appliances intelligent, to colonizing space. If just one of them is successful, it will blow our minds and change the world.

Some are dreaming of solar power in space, where there is no night and no atmospheric gases or clouds ever block the sun. Some sort of microwave transmitter or laser would direct energy to the areas of earth that need it. But we would probably need big breakthroughs in telerobotics to build and maintain solar panels in space.

Closer to home, others are working on an internet for energy – an intelligent and decentralized network of power lines, sensors and switches where both producers and consumers can put information and power into the network, and take it out. Appliances would shut themselves off when they were not needed or when energy was scarce, so the dishwasher might start in the middle of the night. This might also help solve the storage problem from solar and wind power, since energy that is not used could be stored in appliances, cars and homes. You could charge your car when electricity prices were low and send it back to the grid when prices were high.

Many companies are working on artificial photosynthesis, where no organism is needed to turn sun, water and CO_2 into 'solar fuel'. Others are genetically modifying bacteria to make them eat waste and excrete crude oil. The geneticist Craig Venter is experimenting with designer algae, where you can decide whether you want gasoline, diesel or jet fuel, and then just give the algae the relevant DNA instructions.

Several scientists are working on ways of removing CO_2 from the air. It might sound far-fetched, but after all, this is what trees do every day. So far it is incredibly expensive, but technologies change, and it would be one way of not just reducing, but actually reversing global warming. A great benefit would be that the machines don't have to be close to the source of the emissions, so they can be placed where energy is the cheapest and where it is easy to store and make use of the carbon dioxide.

No one person knows what is going to work out in the end. That is why we need more knowledge, more experiments and more collaboration. If the progress described in earlier chapters has taught us anything, it is that development comes from more brains having access to more knowledge, and more eyeballs looking at problems and trying to fix them.

As the spread of electricity and the internet connects us, more people learn about what is going on in the world and get the tools to participate. I have had the pleasure of watching young boys and girls in Moroccan villages get access to electricity for the first time, as they take their first steps online. They are about to enter a global world. Not only can they learn to read and write; they now have access to the sum of humanity's knowledge, and can add their own ingenuity to it. The problem at the heart of global warming – our thirst for energy – is, in fact, also the solution.

7

LITERACY

The mind is not a vessel that needs filling, but wood that needs igniting.

Plutarch[1]

When Lasse Berg and Stig Karlsson met the poor agricultural worker Bhagant in the Indian village of Saijani in 1977, Bhagant did not know that he lived in India. At first, he thought that the photographer, Karlsson, had a problem with his eye, since he always had to hold a machine to it. His daughters, who were eight and twelve, worked hard in the home, in the fields and with the farm animals. Bhagant was a *dalit*, and none of the lower castes in his village got an education. They could not follow the news, learn about other places or make themselves heard. Partly as a result, they lived in abject poverty.

As we saw in chapter 4, this story has a happy ending. When Berg went back in 2010, he returned to a literate village. In Bhagant's generation almost no one got an education; in his children's generation some got an education (though not his children); in his grandchildren's generation almost everyone does. People follow news on the internet and walk around with mobile phones, and see themselves as part of a bigger world.

They discuss wars on other continents and global prices. Bhagant now owns a tractor, and his grandson uses it to work for bigger farmers. His granddaughter Seema will never work on the land – she is becoming a computer technician.

When I have visited different Indian cities I have always been struck by the frequent sight of large groups of children in uniforms walking to and from school. Since India's independence in 1947, the literacy rate has increased from twelve to seventy-four per cent – which still gives India the largest illiterate population in the world. The youth literacy rate – literacy among those aged fifteen to twenty-four – is now more than ninety per cent.

Literacy has given a new generation of Indians access to information and a voice in society. It has made it possible for them to pick up new skills and ideas, to get better jobs and to become more independent of big landowners. But Bhagant also has a complaint. With better education, the young don't know their place. They contradict their parents and complain about their situation. They are not content any more. They want more from life. As Berg points out, 'Mostly this is about villagers raising their focus from the furrow they ploughed for generations, to start to gaze with curiosity at the world a little further away. They have started to dream.'[2]

Literacy – the ability to read and write texts – is one of the most important skills, since it is the capacity to acquire even more capacity. It makes it possible to make much greater use of knowledge that others have. This often reduces poverty directly since it makes it possible to pick up skills and ideas that make you more productive and able to use technology better. It is also important in order to be an active and informed citizen and to follow and participate in the world of knowledge and

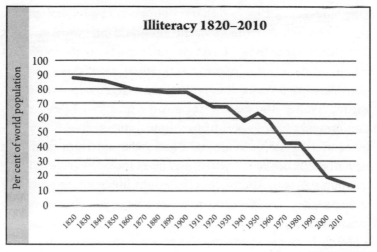

Source: OECD 2014.[3]

entertainment. It has been shown to have a very strong influence on one's health and the health of one's children.

Two hundred years ago, according to the OECD's best estimate, twelve per cent of the world's population could read and write.[4] Until then, literacy was mostly a tool for the bureaucracy, the Church and the merchant class. Along the Asian Silk Road and European rivers and across the Saharan desert, traders developed and used letters and numbers to keep track of supplies and deals. In some northern European countries universal reading skills had been encouraged by the Church since the Reformation, but that was mostly for reading religious texts, and did not always include writing. Most schools were run by the Church, and focused on religious education.

Many in the European élite thought it would be dangerous if the poor got an education. They might become unhappy with their lives and stop accepting their lot in life. But during the early nineteenth century, charity groups and philanthropists started schools for the poor in countries like Britain, and Parliament began to devote funds to that purpose. In the 1870s, elementary education became compulsory, and poor parents were exempted from paying fees. The general public were already open to the idea of expanded education. Even before elementary school was made compulsory and free, 95.5% of school-aged children in England and Wales were enrolled in a school, according to a Royal Commission study.[5]

Literacy is what's known as a classical relational good – the more people who can read and write, the more you stand to benefit from being able to read and write. And if a sufficient proportion is literate, business and culture is transformed so that it becomes punishingly difficult to participate in society if you are illiterate. In most societies, as literacy becomes more broad-based, the trend becomes self-sustaining. In Sweden as early as 1631, Anders Bure wrote that the inhabitants in Norrland, the sparsely populated northern part of Sweden, 'are so fond of letters, that, although public schools are very few, nevertheless the literate instruct the others with such enthusiasm that the greatest part of the common people and even the peasants are literate'.[6]

Progress in literacy has followed economic development quite closely. In western Europe, the United States and Canada, increasing incomes and formal schooling for the masses meant that around ninety per cent of children attended school in the late nineteenth century. By then, the large majority had basic literacy and numeracy skills. It took another half-century before the same was the case in eastern Europe, Italy and Spain.

The spread of literacy came later in countries that industrialized later, but as in previous chapters, it came about faster. In the early 1900s, a few developing countries like Chile, Cuba and Argentina could brag about a fifty per cent literacy rate, but countries like India and Egypt remained below ten per cent. Whereas the attainment of literacy often predated state school systems in northern Europe and North America, formal schooling played a much greater role in the rest of the world.

In 1900, less than ten per cent of the population in South Asia, the Middle East and sub-Saharan Africa had received basic education. By the 1990s, around half had. Today it is around seventy per cent. Even in sub-Saharan Africa, it is sixty-five per cent. In Latin America, the proportion increased from twenty-three per cent in 1900 to ninety-four per cent in 2010. In East Asia, from thirty to ninety per cent. The average time children spend in school increased from a world average of 3.2 to 7.7 years between 1950 and 2010. This is higher than the Swedish average in 1950.[7]

The global literacy rate increased from around twenty-one per cent in 1900 to almost forty per cent in 1950, and in 2015 it was eighty-six per cent. This means that today, only fourteen per cent of the global adult population *can't* read and write, whereas in 1820 only twelve per cent *could*.[8] Despite inequalities, this means that we have seen rapid convergence. Poor countries used to have only one-eighth of the literacy level of rich countries; now, it is half.[9]

Some of the most astonishing achievements are very recent. Since 1990, primary school enrolment in low- and middle-income countries has increased from eighty to ninety-one per cent. In southern Asia, it increased from seventy-five to ninety-five per cent and in northern Africa from eighty to ninety-nine per cent. The United Nations considers a threshold of ninety-seven per cent to represent universal enrolment. By that standard, it has been reached or is close to being reached in all regions except sub-Saharan Africa. But the rate has increased more there than anywhere else, from fifty-two to eighty per cent since 1990.[10] Considering the fact that very few African countries had attained primary enrolment rates above five per cent before the Second World War, this is a remarkable feat.[11]

The number of out-of-school children worldwide has fallen from 100 million to fifty-seven million between 1990 and 2015, despite a much larger population. More than half of them live in sub-Saharan Africa, since income is one of the strongest correlates of enrolment. In developing countries around twenty-two per cent of school-aged children in the poorest quintile are out of school, but only 5.5% in the richest quintile. And the risk that the poorest do not complete primary school is about five times higher than for the richest.[12]

As late as 1970, half the adults in developing countries were illiterate. Today, less than a fifth are. Today illiteracy mostly exists among older people who never got an education while they were young. 'Illiteracy is rapidly becoming a curable condition of youth rather than a chronic condition of adulthood worldwide', as the development economist Charles Kenny puts it. In 2015, the global youth literacy rate was ninety-one per cent, an increase of eight percentage points since 1990.[13]

Whereas formal schooling has made the biggest difference, in some places mass literacy campaigns, which aim for a broad-based improvement in the literacy skills of adults, have resulted in big one-off improvements. This was often a means of promoting national unity, and most often had an impact straight after independence or a major political transition. 'If you know, teach; if you don't know, learn', a Somali campaign urged its citizens in 1974, and the public responded brilliantly: literacy increased from five to twenty per cent. Thailand's first national campaign, in 1942–5, taught 1.4 million people to read. With the help of European development aid, Tanzania's government almost doubled the literacy rate between 1967 and 1975.[14]

Higher incomes and more peaceful conditions have supported education. The only time we have seen a global decrease in literacy since 1820 was during the Second World War. Development has also given parents an incentive to school their children. If there is a greater chance that your children will live a long life, with opportunities of finding well-paid jobs, it makes more sense to spend resources on giving them several years of schooling. As Kaushik Basu, then an adviser to India's government, pointed out in 2012, most of India's rapidly increasing literacy rate is the result of parents deciding to spend more directly on their children's education: 'Ordinary people realised that, in a more globalised economy, they could gain quickly if they were better educated.'[15]

This often happens through private schools – almost a quarter of Indian children now go to private schools that charge a small fee. Parents are willing to pay for this since the public schools often suffer from the same corruption that plagues the political system, and a lot of money is wasted. An inspection of rural schools in India in 2010 showed that a quarter of teachers were absent. Pakistan recently discovered that it was paying for more than 8,000 schools that did not exist – accounting for seventeen per cent of the country's schools.[16]

James Tooley, a British professor of education policy who has researched private education all over the world, claims that parents are most often better placed than governments to decide on their children's education. He has met parents in Asian and African slums who talk to everybody they meet about which schools are the best and visit schools until they find the right one. And when they find a school that is better, they move their children there, which forces private schools to work hard to deliver the best education. Sometimes a government creates public schools that provide almost no proper education just to impress donor countries with enrolment rates, but private schools have to show results to get the children to stay.[17]

Girls have benefited the most from the expansion of education, because they were universally the most discriminated against. Just as the ruling classes feared the enfranchisement of the poor, men feared that if women read, they would develop too much independence. (Interestingly, in the sixteenth century, publishers began to offer smaller versions of books so that they could be hidden from husbands.) When Sweden created a national six-year-long primary education in 1842, one prominent priest in Parliament wondered why girls were being included. What use could they have for writing, except possibly writing the odd love letter to a fiancé? he asked.

The opposition to education for girls is still widespread in reactionary and fundamentalist circles. The Taliban banned girls in schools when they ran Afghanistan, and girls and teachers in underground schools risked execution. The Pakistani Taliban even tried to kill fifteen-year-old Malala Yousafzai for her promotion of education for girls in the Swat Valley. But in most countries around the world, female participation is rapidly approaching that of their male counterparts. The global ratio of female literacy to male literacy increased from fifty-nine to ninety-one per cent between 1970 and 2010. In the youth group, those aged fifteen to twenty-four, it is almost ninety-six per cent of male literacy.[18]

The ratio between the primary, secondary and tertiary enrolment rate of girls and boys was around 0.8 in 1990 for low- and middle-income countries. By 2015, this had increased to 0.98 for primary and secondary education and 1.01 for tertiary education.[19] This is an astonishing accomplishment, and important not just for justice and equal opportunities, but also because child mortality falls as women's level of education increases. Part of this can be explained by the fact that education often leads to a job, a higher income, and better access to food, hygiene, and clean water. However, the effect goes beyond what can be explained by these factors indicating that better-educated mothers will assume more active responsibility for their children's health than those who believe that illness and death are controlled by God or destiny.

Few individuals have borne more powerful witness to the power of literacy than Frederick Douglass, the African-American slave who later became a celebrated orator and reformer. In 1838, at thirty years old, he escaped captivity by jumping on a train to the North, and ended up in New York. He was overwhelmed, and could not even describe his happiness: 'Anguish and grief, like darkness and rain, may be depicted; but gladness and joy, like the rainbow, defy the skill of pen or pencil.'[20]

Douglass's emancipation had begun when he taught himself to use that pen and pencil. The wife of the slave-owner, Hugh Auld, had taught him the alphabet, but Hugh had disapproved, worrying that a literate slave would not be content with his station in life, and would begin to demand freedom.

Douglass took every chance to leave the 'mental darkness' of his early life. He made friends with young white boys he met in the streets and got them to help him understand the meaning of letters and words. When he was sent on errands, he always took a book with him, got the errand out of the way quickly and found time for a lesson before he had to return. Later on he taught himself to write, by telling every boy he met that he could write as well as they, and challenging them to contests. As the boys wrote letters, he copied them, on the board fence, brick wall and pavement, with a lump of chalk.

It turned out that the slave-owner, Hugh Auld, was right. Learning to read and write allowed Douglass to understand his situation, and he began to deplore slavery. Douglass has said that as he learned to write, he began to see himself as himself, rather than through the eyes of the slaveholder. By reading books and newspapers in secret he learned that there were states where blacks were free, and that there were whites opposed to slavery. He learned about slaves who had escaped and began to plan for it himself. He even began to teach other slaves on the plantation to read at a secretive weekly school.

Frederick Douglass claimed that literacy set him free. But at times, before he had escaped to freedom, he saw it as more of a curse than a blessing, because it made him see his horrible condition without granting him the remedy. It created an insatiable thirst for liberation:

The silver trump of freedom had roused my soul to eternal wakefulness. Freedom now appeared, to disappear no more forever. It was heard in every sound, and seen in every thing. It was ever present to torment me with a sense of my wretched condition. I saw nothing without seeing it, I heard nothing without hearing it, and felt nothing without feeling it. It looked from every star, it smiled in every calm, breathed in every wind, and moved in every storm.[21]

8

FREEDOM

History is little else than a tableau of human crimes and misfortunes.

Voltaire[1]

When Frederick Douglass was around ten years old, his slave-owner died. Since he had left no will, his property had to be valued and divided between his son and daughter. Frederick and the other slaves were immediately sent for. All were lumped together, men and women, old and young, married and single. 'There were horses and men, cattle and women, pigs and children, all holding the same rank in the scale of being, and were all subjected to the same narrow examination.'

But this total dehumanization of young and old was nothing compared to the horror of division:

Our fate for life was now to be decided. We had no more voice in that decision than the brutes among whom we were ranked. A single word from the white men was enough – against all our wishes, prayers, and entreaties – to sunder forever the dearest friends, dearest kindred, and strongest ties known to human beings.[2]

And the slaves knew very well that if they ended up in the wrong hands, the hands of a more brutal owner, there was no limit to the horrors they could be put through, from dawn till dusk.

Slavery is the most brutal form of oppression the world has known. Chattel slaves were the property of someone else, who could order them around, beat them at will, give them away or rent them. And the condition used to exist everywhere. In fact, slavery used to be so common that even the few vocal opponents of slavery often owned slaves. They were forced to perform everyday chores and crafts, to work on the fields or down mines, and they were forced into prostitution.

Dick Harrison, a Swedish historian who has written a landmark history of slavery, says that he has yet to find an example of a civilization that did not at some point practise slavery. In academia and in popular debate we tend to focus on particular, modern varieties of slavery, such as the Atlantic slave trade, as I do here, but slavery has always been with us. Between thirty and sixty per cent of Africans were slaves before the Europeans took control of the slave trade there, taken by Arabs or other African tribes.[3]

In the Bible, slavery is considered a natural, established institution. In the Old Testament, we learn that 'You may treat them as your property, passing them on to your children as a permanent heritance' (Leviticus 25:45), and in the New Testament slaves are told to 'obey your earthly masters with deep respect and fear. Serve them sincerely as you would serve Christ' (Ephesians 6:5).

Slaves in Ancient Sparta outnumbered free individuals by seven to one, according to the Greek historian Herodotus. Even in democratic Athens there were probably more slaves

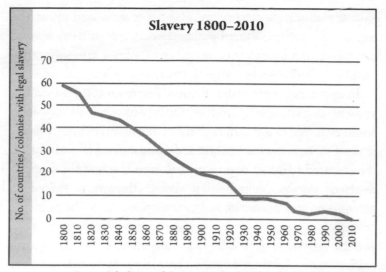

Source: 'Abolition of slavery timeline', *Wikipedia*, 20 February 2016.

than free men. It was a sign of utmost poverty not to own at least one slave and the literature is filled with scenes where slaves are flogged for disobeying their masters. In Roman times there were slave markets in every city of the Empire, and wealthy families could hold hundreds of slaves. Julius Caesar brought slave traders with him on his campaigns and sold prisoners directly on to them. In his *Gallic War*, we learn that when he defeated the Aduatuci, a Germanic tribe, he sold all 53,000 survivors as slaves on the spot. The slaves seem to have lived an extraordinarily difficult life in brutal circumstances, often with severe punishments when they did not please their masters. The average life expectancy for slaves in Rome might not have been higher than seventeen years.[4]

European powers routinely enslaved colonial populations, and gave a religious justification for it. In 1452, Pope Nicholas

V gave Catholic countries 'full and free permission to invade, search out, capture, and subjugate the Saracens and pagans and any other unbelievers and enemies of Christ wherever they may be . . . and to reduce their persons into perpetual slavery'.[5]

As Spain and Portugal took control of America in the 1500s, indigenous people were oppressed and enslaved. There were a few brave opponents to this practice though, the most prominent of whom was the Spanish Dominican friar, Bartolomé de las Casas. He argued that indigenous people had the right to their own persons, beliefs and properties, making Las Casas an early proponent of human rights theory.

But it is not easy to set yourself apart from the period in which you live. Even this man, who spent fifty years of his life fighting against slavery, found it difficult to explain how a world without slavery would work. As an alternative to enslaving the Indians, Las Casas suggested that Spain could import African slaves to the American plantations. He came to regret this, and concluded that Africans had the same individual rights as the Indians, but this horrible system survived him by more than 300 years. Unlike the indigenous population, African slaves could be continuously replaced by new slaves from Africa as they died, and they became an integral part of the American economy. Perhaps as many as ten million people were taken in the Atlantic slave trade, and the conditions were as brutal as the world had ever seen. Africans were kidnapped and marched to the coast, where they were imprisoned for a long time until a slave ship arrived. Some ten to twenty per cent died in overpacked ships on their way to America, chained by leg irons, handcuffs and neck collars. Perhaps as many as 1.5 million slaves died just on the slave ships.

During the Enlightenment, with its attack on hierarchies and traditions, Las Casas' arguments about self-ownership became widespread among philosophers. Like the Leveller Richard Rumbold, Enlightenment thinkers most often believed in the equality of rights, and rejected the notion that the greater part of humanity was born with saddles on their backs and bridles in their mouths, with some few booted and spurred to drive them. The classical liberals of the Scottish Enlightenment, Francis Hutcheson and Adam Smith, condemned slavery early on, and in 1772 the Chief Justice of England declared slavery illegal. Any slave brought into the country would be set free the moment they set foot in England or Scotland. In Parliament, William Wilberforce fought against the British slave trade and for complete abolition for almost half a century.

The French Enlightenment thinkers also opposed slavery. In the great *Encyclopédia* in 1765, Denis Diderot wrote that, 'This purchase is a business which violates religion, morality, natural law, and all human rights. There is not one of those unfortunate souls . . . who does not have the right to be declared free.'[6]

Voltaire challenged the attitude that slavery was justifiable because the enslaved people belonged to different ethnic groups. In his fictional 1756 *Histoire des voyages de Scarmentado*, Voltaire tells the story of an African who enslaves the white crew of a slave ship: 'You have long noses, we have flat ones; your hair is straight, while ours is curly; your skins are white, ours are black; in consequence, by the sacred laws of nature, we must therefore remain enemies . . . when we are stronger than you, we shall make you slaves.'[7]

Even though this was a conscious, philosophical turning of the tables on the European proponents of slavery, the idea of Africans enslaving whites was not fanciful. For hundreds of years, Europeans lived in fear of the North African Barbary pirates who raided coastal towns to capture hundreds of thousands of prisoners for the Ottoman slave markets in Algeria and Morocco. Parts of the coastal fronts of Spain and Italy were abandoned as a result. In the 1600s pirates began to attack British ships, and families and churches in Britain paid ransoms to set sailors free. One of the reasons why the newly independent United States built a navy was to defend American merchant ships against the Barbary pirates. The United States even fought two brief wars with the Barbary States in the early 1800s.

The president who began to challenge the Barbary States was Thomas Jefferson, and his views on slavery shed light on the United States' tortured relationship with the institution. The Declaration of Independence that he penned in 1776 is one of the most powerful summaries of the Enlightenment worldview, and of humanity's right to liberty. It would seem logical if it also rejected slavery. And indeed it did – in the first draft. One of the British king's crimes listed is the following:

> he has waged cruel war against human nature itself, violating its most sacred rights of life & liberty in the persons of a distant people who never offended him, captivating & carrying them into slavery in another hemisphere, or to incur miserable death in their transportation thither. This piratical warfare, the opprobrium of infidel powers, is the warfare of the CHRISTIAN king of Great Britain, determined to keep open a market where MEN should be bought & sold.[8]

This clause was omitted before it was published. The plantation economy of the American South was too dependent on slavery and the majority of the signatories of the Declaration, including Jefferson himself, were slave owners. The ideals of the revolution could not easily be reconciled with the institution of slavery, and abolition was achieved incrementally. In 1777 Vermont abolished slavery and in 1780 Pennsylvania freed future children of slaves, which became a model for other Northern states, so that slavery was gradually phased out. In 1783, Massachusetts freed all slaves. Over the three decades after the American Revolution, all Northern states had begun to abolish slavery.

In 1806, President Jefferson called for the criminalization of the international slave trade, and the next year Congress voted to make American participation in it a felony. Later the same month, Britain abolished slave trading in the British Empire. How far the climate of ideas had turned against slavery could be seen at the Congress of Vienna in 1815. The victorious powers in the Napoleonic Wars, who were all fairly conservative and fiercely opposed to republicanism and revolution, declared that the slave trade was considered 'by just and enlightened men of all ages, as repugnant to the principles of humanity and universal morality'.[9] Over the next decades almost every European country began to abolish slavery, as did their former colonies in Latin America.

The only country with the will and power to end it globally was Britain. In 1834, slavery was abolished in all the British colonies, and as Britain took more direct control of India, it abolished slavery there in 1843. It formed the West Africa Squadron to patrol the West African coast in search of slave ships. With thirty-six ships after 1845, this squadron was one of the largest fleets in the world. Over more than sixty years, the Royal Navy captured 1,600 ships and freed almost 150,000 slaves, even though some slave traders threw the slaves overboard when they were at risk of detection.

In the United States, the Northern states became ever more hostile to slavery, whereas the system became ever more entrenched in the South. The importation of slaves had been banned, but Southern states were now self-sufficient, with around four million slaves. The situation was always explosive since the balance between free states and slave states in the union was precarious. Officials in the North were obliged to assist slave catchers in hunting down fugitive slaves, but at the same time the hostility to slavery, and the agitation against it, was fierce.

One of the most radical and important abolitionists was William Lloyd Garrison. As a young newspaper apprentice, he had seen many advertisements placed by slave owners who told readers how to identify slaves that had escaped from them. A man with scars in his back from being whipped, someone who had had his small toes cut off, had been injured by a pistol shot or branded on the left cheek. It convinced him what a grave sin slavery was and he started publishing the weekly abolitionist paper *The Liberator*, promising to be 'as harsh as truth, and as uncompromising as justice'. The newspaper always lost money and it nearly bankrupted Garrison, but he kept publishing it for thirty-five years to force Americans to face the moral evil of slavery. For his troubles, a pro-slavery mob tried to lynch him and the Georgia legislature offered $5,000 to anybody who brought him to their state for trial and probable hanging.

Other opponents of slavery created an 'underground railroad' – a vast system of secret routes, meeting points and safe houses that allowed slaves to escape to freedom in Northern states or Canada. At its peak, around one thousand slaves are estimated to have escaped per year.

In the end, it took an anti-slavery president and a brutal civil war to end slavery across the union. When Abraham Lincoln won the presidency on a platform hostile to slavery, several Southern states ceded from the Union, created the Confederacy and seized and attacked federal forts. The Confederacy's vice president Alexander Stephens explained that Thomas Jefferson's idea that all men are created equal was a lie, and that: 'Our new government is founded upon exactly the opposite idea; its foundations are laid, its corner-stone rests, upon the great truth that the negro is not equal to the white man; that slavery subordination to the superior race is his natural and normal condition.'[10]

Southern apologist George Fitzhugh openly talked of the 'Southern Revolution of 1861' as an anti-Enlightenment revolution:

> a solemn protest against the doctrines of natural liberty, human equality and the social contract, as taught by Locke and the American sages of 1776, and an equally solemn protest against the doctrines of Adam Smith, Franklin, Say, Tom Paine, and the rest of the infidel political economists who maintain that the world is too much governed.[11]

But just as this counter-Enlightenment was being fought down in the intellectual arena, it was also defeated militarily. In 1863, President Abraham Lincoln issued a presidential order declaring that slaves in all areas controlled by the Confederacy were to be freed. In February 1865, after the Confederacy had been defeated, Lincoln signed the Thirteenth Amendment to the Constitution, which abolished slavery in the United States.

The anti-slavery bandwagon was seemingly unstoppable. Even the more authoritarian countries followed suit eventually.

Russia freed its serfs in 1861, the Ottoman Empire ended slavery in 1882 and China in 1906. In the next century, Nazi Germany and communist states re-introduced slavery on a massive scale, but they were also the two systems that were most decisively defeated, militarily and ideologically, during the twentieth century. The long arc bends towards emancipation. Slavery has been most persistent in the Arab world, but even there, the last states abolished slavery after the Second World War. Oman abolished slavery in 1970 and Mauritania in 1981, even though it was not criminalized there until 2007.

There can hardly be a stronger example of human progress than the fact that slavery, which existed in almost all countries as late as 1800, is now formally banned everywhere. But this does not mean that slavery is not still practised. Millions still suffer from forced labour, debt bondage, trafficking and forced marriages. Sometimes bans are not enforced by governments, and sometimes it takes place in the informal sector where governments are not able to combat it. The 2014 Global Slavery Index from the Walk Free Foundation estimates that more than thirty-five million people live in modern slavery. The worst offenders are Mauritania and Uzbekistan, where around four per cent of the population lives in some kind of slavery. Islamist terrorist groups like IS and Boko Haram regularly kidnap people to enslave them.

But even though slavery still exists, almost no one defends it on principle any more, so the battle is now a very different one. As Free the Slaves co-founder Kevin Bales puts it:

> Today, we don't have to win the legal battle; there's a law against it in every country. We don't have to win the economic argument; no economy is dependent on slavery (unlike in the 19th

century, when whole industries could have collapsed). And we don't have to win the moral argument; no one is trying to justify it any more.[12]

Another crucial development in the broader emancipation of humanity is the extent to which state power is limited, and rulers are stopped from using government force at their whim. Since the beginning of government, subjects have also fought to restrain it, by limiting and dividing its powers, and by subjecting governments to laws and the popular will. In Europe, the struggle between Church and state limited the reach of either, since this meant that there was another standard by which their rule could be judged. In the Middle Ages, many cities, guilds and communes carved out spaces of freedom from the kings. The Magna Carta of 1215, by which King John of England was forced to give barons protection from arbitrary justice, is the most famous. Just seven years later, the Golden Bull of Hungary introduced constitutional limits on the king, and even included the right to disobey him if he acted against the law.

In the modern era this battle was waged against the royal absolutism of the Stuarts in Britain, the Bourbons in France and the Habsburgs on various European thrones. In the seventeenth century, Enlightenment thinkers like John Locke presented a principled case that monarchs don't have a natural right to rule, and that their right to govern was conditional on them protecting individuals' rights to life, liberty and property. If they did not respect those rights, the people had the right to dispose of their rulers. The Glorious Revolution of 1688 and the American Revolution of 1776 were important milestones, when rulers were replaced by governments that were limited by individual rights and parliamentary control.

The next step in this process was to give people control of the government. Since we are so used to this form of government, it is easy to forget that it is a very recent development. When we look back at the twentieth century, the most important development has been the rise of democracy, argues the Indian economist and Nobel laureate Amartya Sen. It was a slow and tortuous process for centuries, and then suddenly it all happened at once.

In the year 1900, exactly zero per cent of the world population lived in a real democracy, in which each man or woman had one vote. Even the most modern and democratic countries excluded women, the poor or ethnic minorities from elections. New Zealand was in some ways a democratic pioneer, but the indigenous population did not have the right to vote. There were still six years until Finland would allow women to vote. But step by step, more people were included in the democratic process. In the mid-nineteenth century the middle classes and the property-owning farmers had been given the right to vote in western European countries, and the cause of suffrage was taken up by the labour movement, and by women.

By 1950, the share of the world population living in democracies had increased from zero to thirty-one per cent, and by 2000, increased to fifty-eight per cent, according to Freedom House, the civil liberties watchdog. Today, even dictators have to pay lip service to democracy and hold staged elections.

This would have seemed impossible just a few decades ago. In 1975, Daniel Patrick Moynihan was the US envoy to the United Nations and he was worried. Back then, the Soviet Union was strong and had expanded into Vietnam, Cambodia and Laos, and Latin America was ruled by military dictatorships. Greece, the Philippines, Chile and Uruguay had been taken over by authoritarian forces and even India was experiencing a period of dictatorship. At the time, Moynihan wrote that democracy 'increasingly tends to the condition of monarchy in the nineteenth century: a holdover form of government, one which persists in isolated or peculiar places here and there', and concluded that democracy 'has simply no relevance to the future'.[13] At the same time Willy Brandt, the German chancellor, predicted that western Europe had only twenty or thirty more years of democracy left in it.

But then we saw the greatest breakthroughs ever. For more than a decade, dissidents and civil society groups such as Solidarity in Poland, led by Lech Wałęsa, or Charta 77 in Czechoslovakia, funded by the writer Václav Havel and others, had undermined the communist system. They disseminated critical literature underground with the help of photocopiers, and challenged oppression publicly. As resistance grew, what had been open secrets became public facts. People already knew that their governments were oppressive and bankrupt, but now they learned that everybody else knew as well.

When Mikhail Gorbachev became the leader of a stagnating Soviet Union in 1985, he encouraged reform and raised the hope that the Soviets might not respond militarily if the satellite states chose their own path, as they had done in Hungary in 1956 and in Czechoslovakia in 1968. This bred hope. Nationwide strikes in Poland in 1988, and the support of the Catholic Church, forced the government to legalize Solidarity and accept partly free elections in June 1989. The communist party was crushed and the next year, the old dissident Wałęsa was elected president.

At the same time, the communist party in Hungary implemented political reform, and mass demonstrations pushed them to go further. In May 1989, Hungary dismantled its section of the Iron Curtain, and let people escape to the West. In October the Hungarian Parliament adopted legislation for democratic elections. Since thousands of its citizens fled to the West through Hungary, East Germany closed its borders entirely. The imprisoned population protested in ever larger numbers. Every Monday in Leipzig, thousands demonstrated against the dictatorship. The communist leader Erich Honecker ordered the military to shoot protesters, but they refused to open fire on their fellow citizens, and soon the protests attracted hundreds of thousands. Honecker was deposed and in November the regime said it would allow East Germans to travel directly to West Germany through the Berlin Wall. Hundreds of thousands of people gathered by the wall immediately and overwhelmed border guards stood down. They could only watch in surprise as East Germans began to tear down the wall that symbolized their oppression on 9 November 1989. A year later the two Germanys were re-united.

Facing protests, the Czechoslovakian government also gave up in November. After this 'Velvet Revolution', the old dissident Václav Havel became president. The Bulgarian government started a series of reforms and accepted elections in June 1990. Every success inspired people elsewhere, and it started an accelerating chain-reaction. The Revolution of 1989 has been popularly summarized as: 'Poland – 10 years; Hungary – 10 months; East Germany – 10 weeks; Czechoslovakia – 10 days; Romania – 10 hours'. In December 1991, the Soviet Union was dissolved, and fourteen countries declared their independence.

Amazingly, communism had been abolished peacefully. The moment people realized that Soviet tanks would not crush them if they protested, they dismantled communism themselves. The exception was Romania, where crowds booed the dictator Nicolae Ceaușescu at a mass rally he had ordered, and security forces fired on the protesters, until the morning after, when the military switched sides and sent its tanks against the Central Committee. Ceausescu was executed days later.

Many anti-communist dictatorships supported by the United States also realized that patience with authoritarianism was growing thin. In 1989 Brazil saw the first election for president by popular vote since the military coup of 1964. After a fraudulent presidential election in Mexico in 1988, when the computers 'broke down' as the opposition candidate was about to win, political and electoral reforms set the country on the path to democracy. In 1990, Chile's dictator Augusto Pinochet had to step down, having lost a plebiscite in 1988. The same year, South Africa began to dismantle the apartheid system. Countries such as Taiwan and South Korea started serious transitions that turned the dictatorships into stable democracies.

Democracy did not win out everywhere. In China, hundreds of pro-democracy protesters on Tiananmen Square were killed on the same day the Poles crushed communism at the voting booths. In Russia, a chaotic democratic experiment in the 1990s was ended by the increasingly authoritarian president Vladimir Putin. Today we are disappointed that the democratic wave has not gone further, that China is still a dictatorship and that Russia has slid back into despotism. But that is because the events around 1989 and 1990 raised hope and ambition so much that it was always difficult to see how they could be fulfilled. Even so, we have made huge progress since then. In 1990 – *after* the Revolution of 1989 – there were seventy-six electoral democracies in the world – forty-six per cent of all countries. In 2015 there were 125 electoral democracies – sixty-three per cent of all countries.[14]

Democracy has not triumphed everywhere; far from it. But we have learned that it is not impossible anywhere. Looking at the dictatorships in Spain, Portugal, Latin America and the Philippines in the 1970s, it was easy to assume that democracy and Catholicism were not compatible. Twenty-five years ago, many claimed that 'Asian values' made democracy unlikely in Asia, but were proven wrong by countries such as Taiwan, South Korea and Indonesia. Equally, democracy never seemed likely in poor and conflict-ridden Africa. Not a single African country saw a peaceful transfer of power at the ballots in the 1960s and 1970s, and there was only one in the 1980s. But then suddenly, in the 1990s, twelve countries held peaceful elections. Few people thought that it would be possible to abolish apartheid peacefully, but in 1994, Nelson Mandela was elected president of South Africa. Since 1990, more than thirty African governments and presidents have been voted out of office.

In 1959 the political sociologist Seymour Martin Lipset made the case that one important factor that contributes to democratization is increased wealth. He argued that development consolidates democracy, since it increases levels of education and literacy, reduces poverty and builds a middle class. This rising middle class gives energy to civil society and demands certain freedoms. Many have argued against the Lipset hypothesis by pointing to examples of poor democracies, like India, and rich authoritarian states, like Singapore. But even though there are outliers, tonnes of studies and cross-sectional and time-series data from many countries and years reveal a very strong correlation between wealth and democracy.

One classic study found that 'the level of economic development, as measured by per capita income, is by far the best predictor of political regimes'.[15] The most important factor is not that economic development directly results in democratization, but that when a regime changes for whatever reason – it can be the death of the dictator, popular protests or anything else – democracy is far more likely to survive in a fairly wealthy country. At a GDP per capita below $1,500 annually, there is a much greater risk that a new democracy will founder.

But as incomes rise, the chance that a democracy will survive grows dramatically. In fact, the study found that a democracy has never died in a country with a per capita income higher than that of Argentina in 1975 – around $8,000.[16] This might be one reason why the hopes of the Arab Spring were frustrated when new autocrats or civil war replaced the old dictators – those countries were on a much lower level of prosperity when the attempted transition was made.

We have also learned that peaceful mass movements against dictatorships stand a better chance at successful democratic change than violent revolutions, like those we saw during the Arab Spring. If the change has support from insiders, who have the trust of the establishment and the military, as in Spain in 1975 and South Africa in 1988, it makes for a smoother transition. But even though it doesn't help to destroy all institutions and purge every supporter of the old regime, the old guard has to be rooted out. The problem in countries like Russia, Egypt and Thailand is that the old regime stayed in power in a sort of 'deep state', and was always ready to sweep back to power when they felt that the changes were threatening their core interests.

We must also remember that just because many people vote for a song it doesn't mean it's the best one. Governments with majority support can also oppress people. If a population holds deeply anti-liberal views, empowering them might result in more oppression, rather than less. Eighty-eight per cent of Egyptians favour the death penalty for people who leave the Muslim religion, and sixty per cent of Afghans think that relatives are entitled to kill a woman who engages in premarital sex or adultery.[17] What use is democracy in a country where the majority opinion is brutally oppressive?

Increased political participation has sometimes led to such illiberal democracies. In the nineteenth century it often resulted in authoritarian governments in countries that had a tradition of centralized power, such as Prussia and France. On the other hand, it was accommodated smoothly and resulted in an open, dynamic society in places such as Britain and Scandinavia, which had more of a tradition of decentralization, with local governments and councils.

This is one of the reasons why the Arab Spring failed. The countries affected had not yet developed a lively civil society with independent power centres. The strongmen who ruled them for decades did everything they could to suppress independent media, courts and organizations. Therefore, there were no building blocks with which to build an open society. Many citizens found themselves scrambling for protection from chaos and unpredictability by turning either to Islamist radicals or new strongmen, who both fought for total control.

This tells us something important about democracy in the liberal, Western tradition. As the philosopher Karl Popper has pointed out, the idea of liberal democracy is not that the majority is entitled to rule the minority, but that government power is always dangerous and therefore it should always be controlled. Popular control is one of those control mechanisms. Democracy is not a way to sanctify the majority opinion, whatever it happens to be, but to limit the damage any group can do to others, so it has to be combined with the rule of law, rights for minorities and strong civil institutions. Democracy is not there to take us to heaven, but to keep us from hell.

In most instances, democracy has developed in unison with the rule of law and respect for individual rights. Freedom House measures both political rights and civil liberties around the world, based on twenty-five indicators. According to this standard, in 1973 there were sixty-nine countries that were 'not free', thirty-eight 'partly free', and no more than forty-three truly 'free' countries. In 2015, the number of 'not free' countries had been reduced to fifty-one, the number of partly free had increased to fifty-five and the number of free countries had almost doubled, to eighty-nine. The proportion of countries deemed free has increased from twenty-nine to forty-six per cent since 1973, whereas the proportion of 'not free' countries has decreased from forty-six to twenty-six.[18]

One important aspect of liberty is freedom from censorship and the political control of information. The proportion of free countries in this press freedom category only increased from twenty-three to thirty-two per cent from 1984 to 2014, but the major change is that so many 'not free' countries became 'partly free'. The proportion 'not free' decreased from fifty-seven to thirty-two per cent.[19]

Another way of measuring individual freedom is to look at the Economic Freedom of the World, an annual survey from the Canadian Fraser Institute. It measures economic freedom in the broadest sense – the rule of law, impartial courts and the size of government, and people's right to own property, start businesses and trade freely. The global average has increased from 5.3 to 6.9 on a ten-point scale between 1980 and 2013. It has moved from where India was in 1980, before its reforms, to where Taiwan was in 1980, after it had liberalized its economy. If the global average of 1980 appeared as a country today, it would be the 150th freest economy in the world, out of 157 measured, just behind Zimbabwe.[20]

Even though we still have a few classical totalitarian governments in our world, which try to control every aspect of people's lives, such as in North Korea, they are much rarer now. With a more literate population that knows how people in other countries live, this requires a form of oppression that is too brutal to be practicable, so most dictatorships have given their citizens more freedom in their everyday lives in the last few decades. China is still a dictatorship that treats its critics harshly, but there is no comparison to Mao's China, where people belonged to a government work unit that decided what they could do with their lives and even who they could marry or divorce. Back then, even your choice of clothing could get you in trouble with the government.

The Chinese people today can move almost however they like, buy a home, choose an education, pick a job, start a business, belong to a church (as long as they are Buddhists, Taoist, Muslims, Catholics or Protestants), dress as they like, marry whom they like, be openly gay without ending up in a labour camp, travel abroad freely, and even criticize aspects of the Party's policy (though not its right to rule unopposed). Even 'not free' is not what it used to be.

In 1991, economist and Nobel laureate Milton Friedman wanted to end a speech on an optimistic note. He mentioned that a London newspaper 200 years earlier explained that 742 million people were ruled by arbitrary government and only 33.5 million people lived in reasonably free countries. This meant that slaves outnumbered free men twenty-three to one. When Friedman spoke, he updated those numbers by looking at Freedom House's estimates. He said that the unfree still outnumbered the free, but the ratio had fallen to about three to one: 'We are still very far from our goal of a completely free world', Friedman concluded, 'but, on the scale of historical time, that is amazing progress. More in the past two centuries than in the prior two millennia.'[21]

Since Friedman spoke, the ratio has fallen again. Forty per cent of the world population now lives in free countries, according to Freedom House, and another twenty-four per cent lives in partly free countries, including relatively liberal countries such as Mexico and Nigeria. That is more progress in *two decades* than in two millennia.[22]

9

EQUALITY

As man advances in civilization, and small tribes are united into larger communities, the simplest reason would tell each individual that he ought to extend his social instincts and sympathies to all members of the same nation, though personally unknown to him. This point once reached, there is only an artificial barrier to prevent his sympathies extending to all men of all nations and races.

Charles Darwin[1]

Ethnic minorities

The fact that a country is a democracy does not guarantee that it is a liberal democracy that gives individual rights to all its citizens, regardless of ethnicity, religion, gender and sexual orientation. After winning the Second World War against the Nazis' brutal form of racism, the Allied democracies showed how many problems still remained among themselves. When General de Gaulle wanted French troops to lead the liberation of Paris on 25 August 1944, American and British commanders accepted it on the condition that no black colonial forces were included, even though they made up two-thirds of the Free French forces.

Racism has been a natural part of most people's mindset since ancient times and hostility towards (and even enslavement of) other ethnic groups was a regular occurrence. History is one long record of hatred against peoples that were considered inferior. Anti-Semitic pogroms have swept European countries for centuries. In the fourteenth century, Jews were blamed for the plague, and were slaughtered wholesale in many places. When Spain emerged as a unified Christian country in 1492, the first thing the new rulers did was to expel all the Jews who refused to convert. Ten years later, Spanish Muslims were forced to choose between conversion and exile. A hundred years later, the descendants of those who did convert were expelled.

In the sixteenth century hundreds of thousands of Protestants were massacred in France during religious wars. Seventeenth-century Europe was dominated by the Thirty Years' War in which different religious denominations fought for the right to force their religion on others. Even the pioneers of religious tolerance thought that it could not be extended to Catholics, or Protestants, or atheists. There were hundreds of deadly riots against Catholics in England in the seventeenth and eighteenth centuries. Arabs, Europeans and Americans enslaved millions and colonialists appropriated the right to rule, enslave and steal from other peoples. As slavery was abolished in the United States, it was replaced by Jim Crow laws that enforced discrimination against African Americans.

The United States has experienced deadly riots against almost every ethnic and religious minority, including Catholics, Jews and Protestant sects, and Germans, Italians and Irish. In the late nineteenth century there were more than 150 lynch-ings of African Americans per year. As more humanitarian atti-tudes began to take root, ethnic violence was reduced. Deadly riots began to decline in Europe in the mid-nineteenth century and lynchings in the United States began to decline in the late nineteenth century and early twentieth century. They ended, except in isolated cases, in the 1940s and 1950s.

But racism remained a central part of the worldview of some of the most admired and 'progressive' modern statesmen. President Theodore Roosevelt claimed that in nine cases out of ten, 'the only good Indians are dead Indians.' President Woodrow Wilson praised the Ku Klux Klan, cleansed the federal government of black employees, and re-segregated facilities such as cafeterias and restrooms. To separate white and black workers, some federal offices set up screens between them. The young Winston Churchill saw colonial wars as wars for 'the Aryan stock' against 'barbarous peoples', said 'I hate Indians' and was 'strongly in favour of using poisoned gas against uncivilised tribes'.[2] President Franklin Delano Roosevelt, whose first supreme court nominee and his choice for vice president in 1944 were both old Ku Klux Klan members, interned more than 100,000 Japanese Americans in concentra-tion camps, just because they were of the same ethnicity as the enemy.

Evolution has given us an obvious tendency to be kind to and promote the interests of our genetic relations, but it has also endowed us with a tendency to be suspicious of, and even hostile and aggressive towards, those who belong to other families and tribes, and often those instincts are at play when we identify a particular group as different from us. However, the nineteenth-century Irish historian William E. H. Lecky suggested that the advance of civilization and education makes us expand the circle of those whose interest we take into consideration: 'At one time the benevolent affections embrace merely the family, soon the circle expanding includes first a class, then a nation, then a coalition of nations, then all humanity, and finally, its influence is felt in the dealings of man with the animal world.'[3]

The American historian of science Michael Shermer talks about the principle of interchangeable perspectives: our ability to find out how others think, feel and are affected by our behaviour, and our interest in making appeals not just by asserting that 'I am right because I am me', but by appealing to reason and empirical data that apply to everybody. He makes the case that it took some degree of scientific thinking to make such considerations widespread. To change position and put yourself in someone else's shoes is a very complex mental abstraction. Empathy requires contemplation. And the first arguments for tolerance came from Enlightenment thinkers such as John Locke, who wrote in 1689 that 'neither Pagan nor Mahometan, nor Jew, ought to be excluded from the civil rights of the commonwealth because of his religion.'[4]

It is well established in the research on intelligence that humanity is getting better, on average, at abstract problem solving. This is called the Flynn Effect, after its discoverer, James Flynn, and he has illustrated the speed of the change across three generations. When his generation took an IQ test after the Second World War, the average result was 100 points. When his children's generation did the same test in 1972, the average result was 108. When his grandchildren's generation took it in 2002, their average result was 118.[5] This trend seems to hold true in all cultures that have modernized, improved education and developed mass media. Interestingly, the parts of the IQ tests where we perform better are the most abstract ones, where we discover patterns and solve novel problems.

The psychologist and cognitive scientist Steven Pinker has talked about a 'moral Flynn Effect', where our increased ability to abstract from the concrete particulars of our immediate experience makes it possible to take in the perspective of others. One example is how Flynn and his brother tried to get their father to give up racial prejudices by using a thought-experiment. They asked him, 'What if you woke up one morning and discovered your skin had turned black? Would that make you less of a human being?' Their father shot back: 'Now, that's the stupidest thing you've ever said. Who ever heard of a man's skin turning black overnight?' Their father was not stupid, but he was bound to a concrete way of thinking which had no room for hypothetical worlds where we explore consequences and rethink moral commitments.[6]

Additional factors behind increased tolerance are open markets and rising affluence. As Voltaire pointed out, at the Royal Exchange in London the Jew, the Muslim and the Christian transacted with and trusted each other and each gave the name infidel only to the bankrupts. Adam Smith and the classical economists showed that the economy does not have to be a zero-sum game. If all transactions are voluntary, no deal is ever made unless both sides believe they will benefit. In a commercial transaction, foreigners and ethnic and religious minorities are not necessarily our enemies, since we do not have to fight them or discriminate against them to protect ourselves.

None other than Karl Marx and Friedrich Engels pointed out, in the *Communist Manifesto*, that free markets and free trade, 'to the great chagrin of Reactionists', tore down feudal ties and nationalist sentiments:

> All fixed, fast-frozen relations, with their train of ancient and venerable prejudices and opinions, are swept away, all new-formed ones become antiquated before they can ossify. All that is solid melts into air, all that is holy is profaned, and man is at last compelled to face with sober senses his real conditions of life, and his relations with his kind.[7]

Historical research by Harvard economist Benjamin Friedman has shown that periods of economic progress in the United States and Europe have generally been conducive to tolerance, openness and equal rights, partly because the majority do not feel that other groups have to be held back for them to progress. At the same time, periods of low growth have brought intolerance, discrimination and racism, since, in a time of limited resources, each group's success is regarded as a threat to the position of the others.[8]

The political scientist Ronald Inglehart concludes something similar from his decades of research into changing global values:

> Individuals under high stress have a need for rigid, predictable rules. They need to be sure of what is going to happen because they are in danger – their margin for error is slender and they need maximum predictability. Postmaterialists embody the opposite outlook: raised under conditions of relative security, they can tolerate more ambiguity; they are less likely to need the security of absolute rigid rules that religious sanctions provide. The psychological costs of deviating from whatever

norms one grew up with are harder to bear if a person is under stress than if a person feels secure.[9]

It was probably no coincidence that the African American civil rights movement won out in the United States in the 1960s. More than two decades of rapid economic growth had given people a better life. Average life expectancy had increased by thirty years since 1900, and the literacy rate had increased from fifty-five to just under ninety per cent. In just twenty years, the African American poverty rate had decreased from seventy-five to forty per cent. Black athletes and musicians were now leading figures in popular culture.[10]

This progress made the government-imposed segregation and the disenfranchisement of blacks that Southern states implemented after the end of slavery seem ever more anachronistic and unbearable. This American apartheid has been described thus:

> The races were strictly separated by law on streetcars, buses, and railroads; in schools; in waiting rooms, restaurants, hotels, boarding houses, theatres, cemeteries, parks, courtrooms, public toilets, drinking fountains, and every other public space. The mania for separation went to such lengths that Oklahoma required separate telephone booths for the two races: Florida and North Carolina made it illegal to give white pupils textbooks that had previously been used by black students. Macon County, Georgia, took the price for absurdity by seriously debating a proposal that the country maintain two separate sets of public roads, one for each race, and rejecting the idea only because of the prohibitive cost.[11]

A few steps had already been taken by the government. President Truman had desegregated the armed forces and ended discrimination in federal employment. In 1954 the Supreme Court desegregated public schools, and when the Arkansas Governor called out the National Guard to stop Little Rock Central High School from accepting nine black students, President Eisenhower sent federal troops to the high school to protect the students.

But the major steps towards racial equality were taken by the African Americans' own civil rights movement. On 1 December 1955, forty-two-year-old Rosa Parks refused to go to the back of a bus in Montgomery, Alabama, which was the space the law had reserved for African Americans. She said that she was tired after a long day. The police took her to jail.

A group of black community leaders protested by organizing a bus boycott. They chose the twenty-six-year-old Martin Luther King Jr. as their spokesman, a Baptist minister with a gift for oratory. He was ordered to pay a fine, for defying a state anti-boycott law. But this did not deter him. He would go on to be jailed fourteen times, he would be stabbed, have his home blasted by a shotgun and bombed, and would see a motel where he stayed bombed too. Whatever happened he would carry on with a campaign of peaceful civil disobedience, inspired by Henry David Thoreau and Mahatma Gandhi, and explained that America was founded on the Jeffersonian ideal that all men are created equal, with the same inalienable rights, and this must include blacks. In the end, he would be assassinated.

The movement's calm and dignified protests, carried to all Americans' living rooms thanks to a novelty, television, exposed the brutality of Southern mayors and sheriffs who ordered attacks on demonstrators and looked the other way when the

Ku Klux Klan beat them up. The attention the civil rights movement gave the issues resulted in victories. In June 1956 a federal
court struck down bus segregation, in 1964 President Lyndon
Johnson signed the Civil Rights Act banning segregation, and
in 1965 the Voting Rights Act put an end to the ruthless methods Southern states had used to block African Americans from
voting.

Changing attitudes were both a cause and an effect of this
change. In the late 1950s, only five per cent of white Americans
approved of interracial marriage. In 2008, almost eighty per
cent did. In the 1940s sixty to seventy per cent of white
Americans thought that black and white students should go to
separate schools, and as late as the early 1960s, almost half of
white Americans said that they would move out if a black family
moved in next door. Today, almost no one agrees.[12]

One of the largest ideological shifts of the last few decades
has been the acceptance of interracial dating. In 1987, only
forty-eight per cent of Americans thought that 'it's alright for
blacks and whites to date each other', and forty-six per cent
disagreed. In 2012, public approval stood at eighty-six per cent.
In this case, there is a huge generation gap. Only sixty-eight per
cent of the over sixty-fives approve, but ninety-five per cent of
eighteen- to twenty-nine-year-olds do.[13]

Unfortunately, democracy does not always breed tolerance,
since majority groups often use their political power to discriminate against minorities. And in some poor countries, discrimination can increase after democratization, if prejudices are
widespread. On the other hand, wealth, education and an open
debate make a difference. The decline in discrimination began
with de-colonization and with the success of the civil rights
movement in the United States in the mid-1960s. This inspired

a similar trend in other affluent democracies, where ethnic minorities began to demand their rights.

Political scientists Victor Asal and Amy Pate have looked at discrimination against 337 ethnic minorities in 124 countries since 1950 and conclude that the last half-century has seen a significant improvement in the treatment of minorities, with respectful attitudes becoming the 'global norm'. In 1950, forty-four per cent of the world's states had policies of political discrimination against at least one ethnic group. In 2003, this had declined to twenty-five per cent. In 1950, thirty-two per cent had policies of economic discrimination in place. By 2003, this had declined to fourteen per cent. Asal and Pate conclude: 'While there are important regional differences, everywhere the weight of official discrimination has lifted. While this trend began in Western democracies in the late 1960s, by the 1990s it had reached all parts of the world.'[14]

Hate crime is still common. After Islamist terrorist attacks like 9/11, many Muslims and mosques in Western countries have been harassed and attacked. But historically, the most notable thing is that we never saw the kind of broad anti-Muslim riots that might in other eras have been condoned and even supported by a majority of society and its authorities. Hate crime is now actively combated by authorities in all developed countries.

It took a long time to get here, but once the circle of tolerance and respect has expanded, it is difficult to shrink it again. Once you begin to think of Catholics or Africans principally as human beings with individual rights, it is difficult to reconstruct the illiberal view. It is still possible, as was made clear by the Holocaust, which took place in one of the richest and best-educated countries of the world less than a century ago. If openness, wealth and a sense of security contribute to a sense of tolerance and respect, their reversal can result in new hostilities and conflicts. Unfortunately a sense of immediate threat and the demonization of other groups can play to our evolutionary instinct to seek security in our own group, and behave aggressively towards outsiders.

Women's rights

For most of recorded history, women were more or less the property of their fathers, until they married and became the property of their husbands, as symbolized in the wedding ceremony where the father delivers the bride into the hands of the groom. Women did not have the right to vote, own property, control their own bodies, get an education or work outside the home. They could even be bought and sold, like chattel.

This is the other side of our hostility to outsiders: man's ancient attempt to control what he considers his. In almost all societies men have attempted to control the sexuality of women of reproductive age with veiling, chaperoning, purdah, foot binding and imprisonment. Women have been forced to wear chastity belts and undergo genital mutilation. They have been promised away as brides without having any say. In the Middle Ages, the Christian Church sanctified commitments made by girls as young as seven. In China and Taiwan, until after the Second World War, parents could even acquire infant girls to provide a bride for their son, and raise her to the role.

This male proprietary psychology is reflected in the view of adultery, which has been defined in almost every culture in terms of the woman's marital status, since it was considered a property rights violation. Infidelity in a wife was always grounds for divorce, but rarely in a husband. And a man who killed after having discovered a wife's adultery deserved a reduced penalty not just according to Anglo-American common law, but also, for example, Native American, European, Oriental, African and Melanesian law. Until the second half of the twentieth century, Anglo-American law allowed the husband to confine his wife against her will and to rape her at will. Relatives who protected a fleeing woman could be charged with harbouring an eloped wife.[15]

The Enlightenment began to change attitudes to women and for the first time systematically defend their rights. Thinkers like Helvétius and Condorcet defended women's rights. They attacked the idea that observed differences in thinking and behaviour between the sexes proved they were innate, and argued that they were the obvious result of discrimination against women. As Herbert Spencer pointed out, if average mental inferiority is the argument to deprive women of liberties, then those women who are of greater ability than average men ought to have greater rights than them.

As early as the 1780s, the English utilitarian philosopher Jeremy Bentham argued for individual freedom for women, including the right to vote, based on the idea that they had interests of their own of which they were the best judges. He thought that arranged marriages equalled slavery and argued in favour of the right to divorce. One of Bentham's lasting achievements was his effect on his disciple, John Stuart Mill, who would go on to influence the debate about women's rights even more.

The English writer Mary Wollstonecraft was one of the earliest proponents of full equality for women, including female suffrage and the right to pursue a career and own property. She practised what she preached and worked as a professional writer without an aristocratic sponsor, which was very unusual for a woman.

Wollstonecraft's book *A Vindication of the Rights of Woman* from 1792 was one of the first feminist treatises. She demanded that women receive an education, in order to develop their faculties, raise children and be real partners to their husbands, rather than objects of amusement. Discrimination against women did not just hold back women, but also civilization in itself: 'Taught from their infancy that beauty is woman's sceptre, the mind shapes itself to the body, and, roaming round its gilt cage, only seeks to adorn its prison.'[16]

In the mid-eighteenth century the Western world experienced a reading explosion, and people began to read novels, with the story unfolding in a character's own words, so that the reader got to hear her side of the story, and understand her thoughts, emotions, suffering and joy. Bestsellers by Rousseau and Samuel Richardson had female protagonists and male readers everywhere began to imagine what a woman's life was like, from the joy of love to the horrors of arranged marriages. Later on, Charles Dickens explained what the British orphanage and workhouse looked like from the perspective of children, Herman Melville told the reader what it was like for a sailor to be flogged and *Uncle Tom's Cabin* forced many to confront the human realities of slavery. It may be that novels made it easier for people to put themselves in other people's shoes and empathize with them even if they belonged to another gender, class or ethnicity, and as a consequence people became more sympathetic to others.

A virtuous circle began to break down barriers during the nineteenth century. A movement in favour of women's rights began to open up some opportunities for education and careers. This in turn made people see that women were often just as able as men, which reinforced the opinion that they should be treated equally. At the same time, having access to greater intellectual and financial resources gave women a louder voice in the struggle.

Often advocates for women's rights took inspiration from their fight for other freedoms. Many argued that women's situation was analogous to that of slaves, as they were treated as property. But as unenfranchised citizens, they also met similar limitations. Elizabeth Cady Stanton and Lucretia Mott travelled from the United States to participate as delegates in the World Anti-Slavery Convention in London in 1840, but found that they were not welcomed by the male leaders. Some said that women's participation in politics was un-Christian and went against British custom. After some debate, pioneers for human rights at the convention told the women that they had to sit in a separate curtained-off section where they could listen, but were not allowed to speak.

That night, as Mott and Stanton walked down Great Queen Street, they agreed that female emancipation needed a more institutionalized defence. One result was the first women's rights convention in Seneca Falls, New York, in 1848, with 300 attendees. The convention ratified a 'Declaration of Sentiments', patterned on the Declaration of Independence. It included a list of demands that would be central to the feminist struggle. The document objected to women being subjected to their husbands, and deprived of the right to vote, own property, get an education or take many jobs. The demand for the right to vote was contested, but the abolitionist orator Frederick Douglass, who participated at the convention and argued fiercely, convinced participants to include it.

At this time, only the most enlightened states had allowed

women even to own and manage their property during the incapacity of their husbands. The next year, the Tennessee legislature claimed that married women should not be allowed to own property because they lack independent souls. The convention's ideas sparked widespread controversy. According to an article in the *Oneida Whig*: 'This bolt is the most shocking and unnatural incident ever recorded in the history of woman-ity. If our ladies will insist on voting and legislating, where, gentlemen, will be our dinners and our elbows, where our domestic firesides and the holes in our stockings.'[17]

Sweden was a pioneer when it came to women's rights, so a timeline of Swedish reforms reveals how long it took for the whole Western world to approach equality. Not until 1845 did sons and daughters have equal inheritance rights. In 1846, trade and crafts professions were opened to unmarried women and in 1864 they were granted the same rights in trade and commerce as men. In 1853, women got the right to work as teachers in primary schools and in 1870 universities were opened to women. In 1858, unmarried women were granted legal majority if they applied for it, but even though married women got the right to control their own income in the 1870s, they were not granted legal majority until 1921. That same year, Swedish women were allowed to vote in the national election on equal terms for the first time.

There were many brave women who fought vocally for suffrage, but there was also a militant part of the movement. One of the British pioneers was Emmeline Pankhurst who, as a child, overheard her father saying, 'What a pity she wasn't born a lad.' Her group started a campaign of direct action in 1903. They were often arrested and many of them were force-fed to prevent their hunger striking. Their sometimes violent tactics attracted attention to their cause, but also lost them sympathy according to some historians. But as the First World War started, most suffragettes put a halt to their activities and began to support the war efforts, which made the public more sympathetic to their cause. As women took on many of the traditional male jobs and roles after men were sent to the front, it became obvious that they were perfectly capable of living as equals. In 1918, women got their vote, limited at first, full in 1928.

A similar development took place on the other side of the Atlantic. The Nineteenth Amendment to the Constitution, regarding female suffrage, was being hotly debated in the summer of 1920. Thirty-six of the states had to ratify it to make it law, but only thirty-five had done so. A special session in Tennessee was the last hope. During the voting session, the vote was at 48-48, when the twenty-four-year-old Harry T. Burn cast the decisive vote. He had made it clear in advance that he opposed reform. But just ahead of the vote, he got a letter from his mother, urging him to vote in favour. And so he did, and thus – by a whisker – female suffrage came to America.

During the second half of the twentieth century, the women's movement in the West, fired up by the example set by the civil rights movement, managed to abolish remaining laws treating women as property. Divorce laws became more equal. After 1973 an English husband who forcibly confined his wife was considered a kidnapper. A husband could no longer claim justifiable provocation if he killed an adulterous wife or her lover, and her family could no longer be charged for harbouring a fleeing wife.

At around this time, the stigma around contraceptives lifted and the invention of the birth control pill in the 1960s began to change attitudes to premarital sex. Abortion rights on many grounds were secured in Britain in 1967 and in the US in 1973.

The movement towards reproductive rights is very recent, as illustrated by the case of marital rape, which was not criminalized in any American state until 1976 and was outlawed in France and Finland only in 1994 and in Germany in 1997.

The Criminal Law Revision Committee of England and Wales in 1984 thought that if a husband forced his wife into sexual intercourse it 'may evidence a failure of the marital relationship. But it is far from being the "unique" and "grave" offence described earlier [when defining rape].' And the Committee argued that prosecution may 'necessitate a complicated and unedifying investigation of the marital history', and could 'drive couples further apart in cases where a reconciliation might have occurred'.[18] In the end, marital rape was criminalized in Scotland in 1989 and in England and Wales in 1991.

During the twentieth century women's liberation also spread to Latin America, Russia and China. Contraception gave women control of when and how often to give birth, and women began to be seen as an integral part of the labour force in most countries. At the end of the century, few countries still upheld political discrimination by law.

In the year 1900, women only had the right to vote in New Zealand. France declared universal suffrage in 1944, Italy in 1946, and Switzerland in 1971. At the start of 2015, women were completely excluded from the political process only in Saudi Arabia and the Vatican. That year, women were allowed to vote and stand as candidates in municipal elections in Saudi Arabia. This was a first step, even though the country's misogynistic laws prevented women from addressing male voters except from behind a screen and banned them from displaying their photographs. And of course women were not allowed to drive a car to meetings or poll stations.

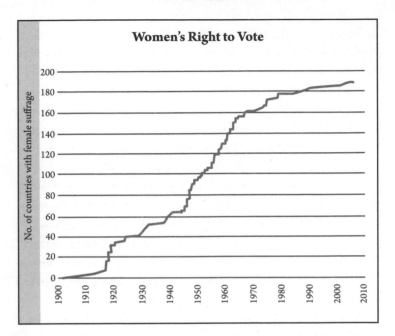

Source: The Moral Arc, Michael Shermer, 2015

The Global Gender Gap Index of 2015, covering 142 countries, produced by the World Economic Forum, gives a glimpse of how far we have come and how far we have yet to go. Globally, almost ninety-six per cent of the gap in health outcomes between men and women has closed, and ninety-five per cent of the gap in educational attainment. But only fifty-nine per cent of the economic outcomes gap and twenty-three per cent of the political outcomes gap have been closed.[19]

The influence that wealth and development has on equality can be glimpsed from the Gender Inequality Index, which is the United Nations Development Programme's way of measuring inequality between men and women in health, literacy, politics and the labour market. Countries with 'very high human development' – the Western world, basically – have an index of 0.197 (where 0 means that men and women fare equally). By contrast, countries with 'high human development' have 0.315; those with 'medium human development' have 0.513; and those with 'low human development' – mostly countries in sub-Saharan Africa – stand at 0.587.[20]

In some regions, very little progress has been made. Ninety-four per cent of Latin American countries have banned domestic violence, fifty-one per cent of Asia, thirty-five per cent of sub-Saharan Africa and twenty-five per cent of the Arab states. The numbers for marital rape are still dismal. It has been banned by eighteen per cent of Latin America, nineteen per cent of Asia, 12.5% of Africa and not a single Arab state.[21]

Similarly, female genital mutilation has been practised for centuries in certain population groups in Africa, Asia and the Middle East. Now it is recognized as a human rights violation by the United Nations and is concentrated in twenty-nine countries in Africa. But even there, it is on the decline. Two-thirds of women and almost two-thirds of men in these countries think it should stop and the risk that a girl will be cut today is about one-third of what it was three decades ago. It is falling out of favour faster in urban areas and among the better-off. In countries such as Ghana and Kenya, the prevalence has declined by three-quarters in thirty years. But since the population is growing rapidly in these twenty-nine countries, the number of girls cut will actually increase, even if the share is being reduced. And the practice continues to affect around ninety per cent of the female population in Djibouti, Egypt and Somalia.[22]

Attitudes in some countries, especially Arabic ones, are still markedly misogynistic. In countries such as Egypt, Iraq, Jordan and Morocco, eighty to ninety per cent agree or mostly agree with the statement 'A wife must always obey her husband.' Sixty-five to eighty per cent think that sons should have a greater right to their parents' inheritance than daughters.[23] The only comfort is that this used to be the majority opinion everywhere in the world until recently.

Attitudes to women's rights have become more progressive for every new generation. When psychologist Jean M. Twenge asked Americans for their opinions on women's duty to obey their husbands, whether their primary responsibility is to be good wives and mothers, and whether women have the same right to act and move about as men, it turns out that men's attitudes today are more feminist than those of women in the 1970s.[24] As late as 1987 only half of Americans thought that it was always wrong for a man to strike his wife with a belt or a stick. Ten years later, eighty-six per cent did.[25]

Every country has its own heroes of female emancipation, some unlikelier than others. Austrian-Ukrainian Beate Sirota moved with her parents to Japan in 1929 when she was six. Ten years later she was sent to college in California, and because of the war she lost contact with her parents. She went back to occupied Japan after the peace as a translator for the US Army, mostly in order to reconnect with her family. One of the US Army's first tasks was to draw up an entirely new constitution in just seven days and Sirota was enlisted to assist. Since she was the only woman on the subcommittee on civil rights, her supervisor thought that she could write the section on women's rights.

It was almost by accident, but she was uniquely suited to the task. She had lived in Japan and had seen how women were treated like property, and had to walk behind their husbands, and she had heard Japanese women complain about how they were bought and sold, like chattel. Therefore she understood that the vote was not enough for women to participate in society; they needed equal rights generally.

She also understood that she needed exact, legalistic language, so that these rights would not be open to misinterpretation or sabotage. So she requisitioned a jeep and went to libraries to look at other constitutions to see how women's rights were phrased there. The result, after a few days with very little sleep, was two unprecedented articles about equality between the sexes, including a women's equal right to choose a spouse, get a divorce, own property and inherit. Because of an enterprising twenty-two-year-old woman, the Americans incorporated an equality clause in the Japanese constitution that had not yet been won in the United States.

For a long time Sirota kept quiet about her role in the drafting of those articles. The work was secret after all, and she was afraid that her youth and gender could be used against the constitutional articles by reactionaries. But in the 1980s she started talking about it publicly, and quickly became a celebrity in Japan. The Japanese government bestowed on her the Order of the Sacred Treasure for distinguished achievements. Whenever she visited Japan later in life, Japanese women would approach her and thank her, with tears in their eyes, for the revolution that she had started.

Gay rights

When Martin Luther King gave his 'I have a dream' speech in Washington, DC in August 1963, six white men stood in the crowd of 250,000 people with signs identifying them as coming from an obscure gay rights group, the Mattachine Society. One of them, Jack Nichols, looked around at the crowd, and asked, 'Why aren't we gays having civil-rights marches too?'[26]

In the early 1960s homosexual acts were illegal in every American state. The Postal Service put tracers on suspected homosexuals' mail in order to collect evidence against them. Gay bars were regularly raided and those caught by the police were not just imprisoned but their names and addresses could also be printed in the newspapers. The authorities would show them gay pornography and give them electric shocks to condition them against it. In some instances they were referred to medical institutions, where they could be sterilized and sometimes castrated and lobotomized.

During the Cold War, homosexuals were often seen as security risks, either because their behaviour made them more susceptible to political radicalism generally or because it made them vulnerable to blackmail, which might make them help the enemy. The rabid anti-communist Senator Joseph McCarthy was among those making a connection between communists and so-called 'cocksuckers' – even though homosexuality was of course illegal in the Soviet Union. Under President Eisenhower hundreds of homosexuals were dismissed from federal employment. Similar purges took place in the British government. Undercover policemen would pose as gay men in public places, and arrested those who took the bait. At the end of 1954, there were 1,069 men in prison in England and Wales for homosexual acts.[27] Someone said that the skies over Chelsea were filled with black smoke with people burning their love letters.

The actions of the American Civil Liberties Union (ACLU) give us some indication of how exposed this minority was.

Many gay people approached the ACLU for legal assistance after suffering discrimination, but it responded that there was 'no constitutional right to practise homosexual acts', and agreed that homosexuals should be excluded from government jobs and the armed forces since, unlike race and religion, homosexuality has a 'functional relevance' to job performance.[28] The feminist icon Betty Friedan thought that lesbians would harm the women's movement, and talked about them as a 'lavender scare' as late as 1969.

After the Second World War, many of the homosexuals who survived the Nazis' concentration camps were actually re-arrested to serve out their terms of imprisonment, under the German ban from 1871. The West German government generally paid reparations to those who had spent time in the camps, but excluded homosexuals. In 1952, the British scientist and war hero Alan Turing, who broke the Nazi Enigma code, was arrested for 'gross indecency', and had to accept chemical castration as an alternative to prison. He committed suicide two years later. He was given a posthumous royal pardon in 2013.

There have always been certain cultures that have tolerated homosexual acts, like the famous relationships between men and youths or slaves in Ancient Greece and Rome, though these patriarchal cultures had a taboo against sex between grown men. Many other cultures condemned all homosexual acts, and the Christian tradition has been remarkably intolerant, often based on passages from the Bible where they are punished with death. In Dante's fourteenth-century *Divine Comedy*, he finds 'sodomites' in the seventh circle – out of nine – of hell, where they have to run forever on burning sand. That is very bad indeed. In the second circle he finds heterosexuals who sinned, which shows that they only failed to show restraint in their natural passions, whereas homosexuals rebelled against God's order by yielding to unnatural passions. They are found in the bottom ring of the seventh circle, beneath murderers.

The Spanish Inquisition stoned, castrated and burned homosexuals and in France first-time offenders lost their testicles and repeat offenders lost their penis. (The third time, they were burned.) In Renaissance Italy homosexual acts seem to have been fairly common, but it was here that for the first time a special organization, the 'Night Officials', were tasked with finding and prosecuting homosexuals. The leading eighteenth-century English jurist William Blackstone pointed out that Ancient English law demanded that homosexuals be burnt to death or buried alive, like the ancient Goths did. Blackstone defended these punishments by invoking Sodom and Gomorrah. But under the English Buggery Act of 1533, homosexual acts were punishable by hanging.

The first signs of a change in attitudes to homosexuality also appeared during the Age of Enlightenment. Jeremy Bentham, who argued for women's rights, also wrote an essay arguing for the decriminalization of homosexuality in 1785. He rejected the idea that it was a threat to society, and concluded that it was a victimless crime, and so should not be considered a felony. The subject was so sensitive that the script wasn't published at the time, but it showed how Enlightenment values and classical liberal attitudes easily turned into an argument for tolerance.

In 1791, Revolutionary France abolished all laws against sodomy and homosexuality and it remained legal under Napoleon's criminal code, although people could still be harassed by the police under laws against public indecency. In the nineteenth century a few other countries began to decriminalize homosexual acts, including the Netherlands and the Ottoman Empire. England executed homosexuals for the last time in 1835, and the death penalty itself was abolished in 1861. Urbanization and industrialization made it possible for people to escape parishes and family traditions and live in less conventional relationships. This made homosexuals more visible, which strengthened the public hostility to them in many places. In 1900, most countries had still banned all same-sex relations, at least for men (since many did not believe it was possible for women to be homosexual), and the European empires brutally suppressed local tolerance in their colonies.

But during the boom years after the Second World War and inspired by other civil rights movements, homosexuals started to organize in the way that Jack Nichols suggested during Martin Luther King's rally. Over the next four years, their Mattachine Society picketed the White House and other government buildings, demanding the same civil rights that all citizens were guaranteed. They were a small group, but they helped to make the community conscious, and their demands visible. By the late 1960s, the ACLU reversed its stance that government discrimination was acceptable, and began to lead the fight against the entrapment of homosexuals, fighting discrimination in the courts.[29]

One hot night in the summer of 1969, the gay movement came out in force, after gay people drinking at the Stonewall Inn in New York got so frustrated by constant police harassment that they responded to a routine police raid with a riot. The widespread media attention galvanized the community, and gay rights groups were founded in many major cities across the US and western Europe. In 1970, Gay Pride marches were held in New York, Chicago, San Francisco and Los Angeles, commemorating the anniversary. Today, Pride is celebrated in cities all over the globe.

In the 1970s, several American states abolished their sodomy laws. In 1973, a federal judge ruled that sexual orientation could not be the sole reason for sacking a federal employee. That same year the American Psychiatric Association removed homosexuality from its list of mental disorders. In 1967, homosexual acts that took place in private in England and Wales were decriminalized, even though the age of consent was higher than for heterosexuals (twenty-one versus sixteen). The young Margaret Thatcher was one of the few Tory MPs who voted in favour. The same reforms applied to Scotland after 1981. However, the privacy restriction meant that people could still be prosecuted if they had sex in a hotel room or if a third person was present in their home. These restrictions were only overturned by the European Court of Human Rights in 2000.

Gay liberation started a beneficial spiral. As more people came out as gay and lesbian, others realized that they were not an alien species, but their relatives, neighbours and colleagues. This created a more tolerant culture, which made it possible for more people to come out, which made the culture even more tolerant, and so on. New gay role models in TV series and on the music scene made an impression. In 1985, only twenty-four per cent of Americans said that they knew someone who was gay. This rose to nearly sixty per cent in the 2000s and to seventy-five per cent in 2013. It used to be odd to know someone who was homosexual, whereas today it is odd *not* to. This represents a very rapid change in attitudes.

Until 2003, when the Supreme Court struck them down, laws banning 'sodomy' remained in fourteen American states. The next year, Massachusetts accepted gay marriage, but this led to a national backlash, and the Republican Party under George W. Bush got social conservatives to the polls in 2004 and 2006 with state anti-gay initiatives and referendums on the ballots. At the time, sixty per cent of Americans opposed same-sex marriage. Indeed, in his 2008 presidential campaign, Barack Obama said that marriage is between a man and a woman and that he opposed gay marriage. But opinion shifted dramatically. In 2014, sixty per cent of Americans opposed gay marriage, and today sixty per cent approve of it. Obama changed his mind in 2012, and Bush has offered to officiate at at least one gay wedding. In 2015, the Supreme Court decided that same-sex couples have the constitutional right to marry.

Just a few decades ago gay sex was illegal almost everywhere. In the Soviet Union, homosexuals were sentenced to five years in prison; in China they were sent to labour camps. Today, it is still illegal in many African countries, Middle Eastern countries and South Asia, but elsewhere it is difficult to find bans. It is legal in at least 113 countries, including China and – despite bans on 'homosexual propaganda' – in Russia. Large majorities in Latin America think that society should accept homosexuality. In countries such as Chile and Argentina more people are tolerant than in the United States.[30] No country accepted same-sex marriage until the Netherlands did in 2001. Today it is accepted in twenty-one countries, including the staunchly Catholic Ireland. Many other countries accept unions that give same-sex couples similar legal protections to marriage.

Still, it is illegal in many countries, and a capital offence in five – Iran, Mauritania, Saudi Arabia, Sudan and Yemen. Some countries, such as Russia and several African countries, denounce homosexuality as a way to distance themselves from the West and liberal attitudes in general. But the historical trend is strong, and the forces that have contributed to tolerance – affluence, education, urbanization, visibility – are at work globally.

Bigotry remains around the world, against women, gay people and ethnic and religious minorities. In a few countries it still has strong official approval, but they are on the wrong side of history. In many more countries people still face prejudice, hostility and hate crimes every day, but now, for the first time, governments are protecting equality and the right to love anyone, and bigots can no longer be certain of the help, or even silent acceptance, of majority communities. That is amazing progress, indeed. The next generation will grow up surrounded by more tolerance and greater acceptance than ever before, to the great chagrin of reactionists.

10
THE NEXT GENERATION

The main fuel to speed the world's progress is our stock of knowledge; the brakes are our lack of imagination and unsound social regulations of these activities. The ultimate resource is people – especially skilled, spirited, and hopeful young people endowed with liberty – who will exert their wills and imaginations for their own benefits, and so inevitably they will benefit the rest of us as well.

Julian Simon[1]

I visit Thi-Chi in her home just outside Ho Chi Min City in southern Vietnam. She looks around her home, at the rice fields all around us. That is where she used to work as a child. From a very young age she had to work there, day in and day out, in the burning sun and in the intense rain. Just like her parents did when they were children, and their parents before them. Not because they were mean or didn't care about their children, but because they were desperately poor and needed the labour of their children in order to feed the whole family.

Parents have been forced to make the same decision everywhere. Child labour was not historically a subject of concern, but a natural way of life. This was always the case, everywhere, in all eras but ours.

In recent times, the public has sometimes held the impression that child labour was a result of the Industrial Revolution, but more recent literature points out that this is because that was the first time when people began to react to child labour, write about it and demand an end to it. As the legendary economic historian Eli Heckscher pointed out:

> the notion that child labour in either theory or practice was a result of the Industrial Revolution is diametrically opposed to reality. Under mercantilism it was an ideal to employ children almost from the age when they could walk, and, for example Colbert [King Louis XIV's statist Minister of Finances from 1665 to 1683] introduced fines for parents who did not put their six-year-old children to work in one of his particularly cherished industries.[2]

In old tapestries and paintings from at least the medieval period, children are portrayed as an integral part of the household economy. Children spun thread for the parents to weave on the loom, they planted seeds and cleared weeds, collected firewood, herded livestock, helped with ploughing, and contributed to all sorts of domestic tasks.

Since we have a somewhat rosy, nostalgic picture of agriculture, this has sometimes been romanticized as a way to learn important tasks in a close family circle. That was certainly often the case, but it is also true that the work was often backbreaking

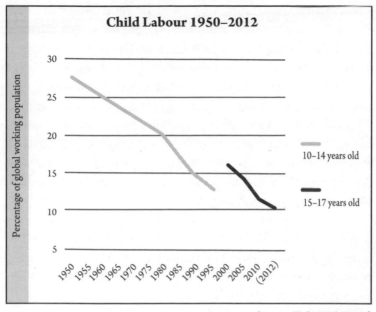

Sources: ILO 1996, 2013.[3]

and stunted children's intellectual development. Children would be beaten when they did not perform the tasks the way parents demanded.

They were also often hired out to work in other families' homes as domestic servants. Often they became totally dependent and lived with strangers. Many worked hard in small workshops and in home-based industry, and some scholars suggest that this was more intense and exploitative than child labour during industrialization. In the worst cases, children climbed chimneys and worked in mines. Prior to the mid-nineteenth century it was common for working-class children to start working from seven years of age. Here, as elsewhere, the survival of the family demanded that everybody contributed.[4]

Far from being considered a problem, child labour was seen as a form of education, and as a way of preventing idleness. When the author Daniel Defoe wrote about the Lancashire cotton industry in 1726, he was happy that children as young as four had found useful employment there. The seventeenth-century Enlightenment philosopher John Locke was a pioneer when it came to championing children's rights, but nonetheless he recommended that the children of the poor be put to work at three years of age. In 1840, the Mayor of Liverpool complained about the 'want of employment' for children, since that led to idleness and plunder.[5]

The extraordinary thing is how ordinary ideas like that were at the time. Childhood was not seen as an enclosed period of innocence, but as a period when young individuals contributed to the household and picked up the skills they needed later in life, side by side with adults.

The major change brought about by early industrialization was that those jobs sometimes moved to factories. Obviously, it seems much worse to send a child away from home to work, and often it was. But it also meant that many children who would otherwise have been sent away to live permanently in other households and farms could now go back home to their parents every night. Widespread criticism of child labour started in England. This may not have been the result of child labour being more widespread and brutal than in other places, but an indication that child labour was starting to be reduced, a trend which brought with it a cultural re-evaluation of the role of children and an opposition to very young workers.

In 1851, twenty-eight per cent of children aged between ten and fourteen in England and Wales were recorded as working. This is a shockingly high number, and it did not even include the numerous girls who were working unpaid at home looking after younger siblings or generally helping out. Yet it is much lower than it was in non-industrialized countries even 100 years later. In 1950, the child labour rate in China has been estimated at forty-eight per cent, in India thirty-five per cent and in Africa thirty-eight per cent. Even in a relatively rich country like Italy the child labour rate was twenty-nine per cent in 1950.[6]

Traditionally, legal restrictions on child labour, such as the British Factory Acts, have been credited with reducing its prevalence, but Clark Nardinelli concluded in a revisionist account of the history that those acts 'did not cause the long-term decline in child labour. Instead, they may have been more an effect of the decline than a cause.'[7] As long as parents were dependent on their children's income for their livelihood, bans were often neglected, and if they had any effect it was that children got more dangerous jobs in the informal sector, sometimes even prostitution or robbery.

What was needed was to reduce the supply and the demand. That came in the nineteenth century in the form of rising wages, universal education and technological change. Rising wages meant that parents were not as dependent on their children's labour as they used to be. At the same time routine jobs in industry were mechanized. This resulted in a reduced demand for children who could perform simple tasks, and an increased demand for skilled adults. Both of these changes increased school enrolment. As children did not need to work, they could attend school, and as the skills premium increased, parents benefited economically by taking children out of work and instead investing in their future skills.

The rate of child labour in England and Wales was reduced from twenty-eight per cent in 1851 to twenty-one per cent in

1891 and fourteen per cent in 1911, and soon it disappeared altogether. Step by step, this happened in every industrialized country. The same change is now taking place in low- and middle-income countries as they go through the same process.

Thi-Chi, the Vietnamese woman from the beginning of this chapter, does not work in agriculture any more. In the early 1990s, when Vietnam's economy was opened up to global trade, the country increased its agricultural exports and received substantial foreign investment. The result has been rapid economic growth. Thi-Chi now has a job in the factory, producing sports shoes for Western markets, making five times more than she used to. This means that she can afford to forgo her son's income and give him a proper education. Smiling, she tells me that she wants him to become a doctor.

Between 1993 and 2006, the proportion of ten- to fourteen-year-olds in child labour in Vietnam was reduced from over forty-five per cent to just under ten per cent. Child labour among six- to nine-year-olds declined by ninety-three per cent over the same period.[8]

These are not just fantastic numbers in their own right, but they also say something interesting about child labour itself. It seems to suggest that parents put their children to work not to maximize income, but because they have no alternative. Rapidly increasing rice exports in the 1990s meant that the value of Vietnamese children's potential work increased, so if parents simply wanted more resources, they would have put their children to work. Instead, the number of child labourers declined by several million in just a few years. This indicates that children only work because their families cannot afford to raise them without help. Parents will remove their children from work as soon as they no longer risk starvation, even where child wages are increasing.

In one study in Ecuador, parents' attitudes were examined by a cash transfer experiment. Families who won a lottery received a cash transfer equivalent to seven per cent of monthly expenditures. The cash was less than a fifth of the income the average child labourer received in the labour market, so they lost substantial money if the children stopped working, but even so, there was a decline of forty per cent among those who won. The impact was biggest among the poorest. Apparently, the question is not whether a family can make more money, but whether they can afford to forgo it.[9]

This implies that parents rarely have to be forced to stop their children from working – indeed, that could make a difficult situation even worse – but the moment they can survive without putting them to work, they remove them from the workforce of their own free will.

Research shows that the extent of a country's foreign trade is inversely proportional to the extent of child labour, because trade creates new jobs and higher incomes. As India's economy was opened up in 1991 there was a rapid fall in child labour, from twenty-five to fourteen per cent between 1987 and 1999.[10]

As late as 1950, it has been estimated that more than a quarter of all the world's children between ten and fourteen years of age were economically active – which means that they produced goods or services, including work in other people's households. In Africa and Asia, almost four out of ten children were child labourers in this sense. Now this global number is certainly less than one in ten.[11]

Since 2000, the International Labour Organization (ILO) regularly estimates the number of children between five and seventeen years old working, based on an increasing number of national-level surveys. The overall picture is one of 'significant progress'. In 2012, there were 168 million child labourers in that age group globally, down from 245 million in 2000, a reduction from 16 to 10.6% of all children. Over just twelve years, there was a forty per cent reduction in the number of girls in child labour, and a twenty-five per cent reduction for boys. The proportion of children between five and eleven years old in hazardous work – work in dangerous or unhealthy conditions that could result in a child being injured, made ill or killed – has been reduced even faster, by two-thirds between 2000 and 2012, from 9.3% to 3.1%.[12]

This transition has gone hand in hand with a new valuation of childhood – both a cause and an effect of the end of child labour, but mostly the result of smaller families and the rational expectation that children will live a longer and healthier life. Children are no longer seen as a resource for the household economy to exploit. Instead they are an investment in the future of the family, and individuals in their own right, who should be given the best conditions for a long and happy life. The flow of resources from children to parents has been replaced with the flow of resources from parents to children. One working-class mother in London remembers how, in her childhood in the 1950s, her father would always get any food left over, but now 'if there's one pork chop left, the kiddie gets it.'[13]

Despite what we see in the news, the conditions of childhood have never been as beneficial as they are today. Consider a ten-year-old girl 200 years ago. Wherever she had been born, she could not have expected to live longer than around thirty years. She would have had five to seven siblings, and she would already have seen at least one or two of them die. The chance that her mother would survive childbirth was smaller than the chance that the present generation will meet their grandparents.

She would have been brought up under conditions we consider unbearable. Her family would not have had access to clean water or a toilet. Chances are that they did not even have a latrine; they would have used a ditch or gone behind a tree. Her surroundings would have been littered with garbage and faeces, contaminating water sources and devastating lives. Her parents would live in constant fear that she would be taken away by tuberculosis, cholera, smallpox or measles – or starvation.

This little girl would have been stunted, skinny and short, since she lived in a world of chronic undernourishment and recurring famine, where people did not get the energy to grow and function properly. This would also have halted her brain's proper development. She would not receive any schooling, and would never learn to read or write. She would certainly have been put to work at an early age, perhaps as a domestic servant in another family's home. In any case, she would have been blocked from almost all occupations, and would be considered the property of her father, until he married her away, at which point ownership would pass to her husband. If he beat her or raped her, there was no law banning it. She would not be able to organize politically to change this, since she would not have the right to vote nor stand for election, no matter where she lived. If she wanted to leave it all behind, there were no cars, buses or planes. The first trains existed, but only to transport coal in parts of England and Wales.

She lived in a brutal world, where the risk of a violent death was almost three times higher than today. England had 300 capital offences on the books, and she would still see corpses displayed on gibbets. Torture and slavery were still common. Peacetime was an intermission between wars. The world had just gone through the Napoleonic Wars, with the whole of Europe and many other parts of the world a battlefield. Any security you had built up could be torn apart in a few days.

Since then, humanity has experienced a revolution in living standards. We have now almost completely solved the problem of hunger and sanitation, which has helped to improve health and more than double life expectancy. In contrast to what many feared, this resulted in smaller families, more literate children and the eradication of extreme poverty. The rising middle class, anticipating longer lives for their children, began to abandon violence as a way of solving private and political conflicts, and it began to pay off to invest in the future. The environment had previously been a low priority because of the daily struggle for survival, but as our lives improved, we began to address the wider world. Wealth and knowledge contributed to Enlightenment ideals and to the advent of democracy and human rights, including rights for women, and for ethnic minorities. This in turn has made it possible for more people to contribute to our stock of knowledge and wealth, making it increasingly likely that the future will be even better.

Humanity has climbed the development ladder. Every major breakthrough has facilitated the next one, but has also reinforced the gains we have already made. Literacy has increased wealth, and that new wealth has also made it possible to extend literacy further. Better access to food and health care has made it possible to work more, so that we can ensure even better nutrition and even better health.

The same ten-year-old girl living today is more likely to reach retirement age than her forebears were to live to their fifth birthday. Even if she lives in one of the world's poorest countries, she has better access to nutrition than a girl in the richest countries 200 years ago. The risk that she will lead a life of extreme poverty has declined from ninety per cent to less than ten per cent. She goes to school just like almost everyone in her generation, and illiteracy will be eradicated during her lifetime. Her parents probably support her so that she won't have to drop out to work. Now she has a good chance of living in a democracy, where women have individual rights and protections. She faces a lower risk of experiencing war than any other generation in human history. Her risk of dying from a natural disaster is ninety-five per cent smaller than it would have been a hundred years ago, and she will not even hear of a major famine anywhere.

Philosophers have always debated whether such progress contributes to happiness. Some have said that psychological well-being is something else entirely than physical and material well-being, and is not affected by it. Even though researchers have started measuring this only recently, there are preliminary results pointing to increasing happiness levels globally. Data from representative national surveys on self-reported well-being since 1981 show that happiness has risen in forty-five of fifty-two countries. The researchers believe that the progress this book has described has been essential:

> Regression analyses suggest that the extent to which a society allows free choice has a major impact on happiness. Since 1981, economic development, democratization, and increasing social tolerance have increased the extent to which people perceive that they have free choice, which in turn has led to higher levels of happiness around the world, as the human development model suggests.[14]

When it comes to the pre-conditions for a good life, the starting point for someone born today is a world away from our ancestors 200 years ago. But perhaps the biggest difference is psychological and intellectual. It is difficult for us even to imagine how limited the worldview was for the average person two centuries ago. Not because they were more stupid, or less interested, or had less human potential, but because they lacked the means. They were not literate, and they did not have access to education, the telegraph, the radio or the internet. The main source of news for this girl 200 years ago would have been what she was told in church, or what her father heard in the pub, perhaps from a foreign visitor. She would have been expected to lead the same kind of life that her mother lived, in the same place, and nothing else would ever have seemed possible to her.

How different the world looks to an individual who can get news instantly about the rest of the world. Soon three billion people around the world will own a smartphone. That is three billion people who each have more computer power in their pocket than the super computers of the 1960s had, with instant communication and access to all the world's knowledge. With just one Google search, they set in motion a series of calculations that takes more computing power than was used by the entire Apollo Programme during its eleven-year project of putting a man on the moon. The Chinese bought more than 400 million smartphones in 2015 alone. This is a population that lived in deep misery and was banned from learning anything from the rest of the world just thirty years ago. Now, it has instant access to knowledge from around the world.

Dramatic progress has opened our eyes, and it has opened our minds. The young see alternatives, and are inspired by possibilities that never would have occurred to their parents and the societies they grew up in. As we saw in Bhagant's village in India, the young are restless and discontent with what they have. They will be difficult and bothersome and they will disturb the order of things, because they will demand more than they have. And they will also have and invent tools we can't yet imagine, using the collective reservoir of human knowledge.

Knowledge has always been a scarce resource, for several reasons: cumulatively, we did not know much about the world; we had not developed the literacy and education with which to make sense of our existing knowledge; we did not have the means of widely disseminating what little knowledge we had. Even the intellectual élite found the transmission of knowledge ineffective. At the beginning of the 1880s, Herbert Spencer, one of the leading thinkers of the time, learned that Immanuel Kant's view of human rights resembled what he himself had been propagating for thirty years. But, not knowing German, Spencer had no way of understanding one of history's most famous philosophers. Something like a decade was to pass before Spencer got hold of an English translation of Kant and was able to start noting down similarities.[15]

Now we know more than ever, we are more literate than ever, and we can find almost anything we are interested in, in just a few seconds. Soon every person in almost every country will have a smartphone or a computer with a connection to almost anyone else on the planet. Considering what humanity has been able to accomplish when only a fraction of us had access to a fraction of that knowledge, and could collaborate with only the people we met and knew of, it is easy to predict that a world without such limitations will unleash incredible creativity.

Using a classic metaphor of science as a collaborative venture, Isaac Newton wrote, 'If I have seen further, it is by standing on the shoulders of giants.' In his era, only a small élite of brilliant scientists lived in this world of connected knowledge, where they could make use of the accumulated knowledge of strangers. Now billions do. This time, we do not just stand on the shoulders of giants, we are all helping each other up.

Despite all the progress we have made, there remain huge economic, social and environmental problems. We still face threats of violence, terrorism, forced migration and nature's unpredictability. But the progress we have made also means that more eyeballs than ever can see humanity's problems, and more brains than ever are inventing possible solutions.

The only way we can get close to a world where we explore all possibilities and use all available knowledge – to invent, to create, to solve environmental problems – is to allow everyone to participate. The living standards we have attained have meant that, as a species, we have a bigger pool of energy and intelligence than ever, which will be used to make our lives even better. In physics, escape velocity is the speed an object needs to break free from the gravitational pull of a body. Mankind is now breaking free from the natural and self-imposed limitations that have always held us down. Humanity has reached escape velocity.

The remarkable change around the world in the last few decades can be documented with a little bit of palm reading. We have met Lasse Berg and Stig Karlsson before in this book, the two travellers who had to abandon their pessimistic worldview after repeated visits to the same Indian village revealed fantastic progress.

When they first visited Sajani they met Sattos, a twelve-year-old girl who worked long hours in the home and in the fields, taking care of the animals. At that time, they took a picture of her hands, already furrowed and worn, prematurely aged by years of toil. When Berg and Karlsson returned to check in on the next generation, they took a picture of the hands of Sattos's thirteen-year-old daughter Seema.[16] Those hands do not look anything like her mother's did at the same age. They are young and soft, the hands of a girl who has been allowed to play and to study. They are the hands of a girl who has not been robbed of a childhood, and is therefore better prepared for adulthood.

Those two pictures represent the change the world has gone through over the last few decades. Seema is not just one girl. There are hundreds of millions of girls and boys like her. They are the best educated generation ever, who will live longer lives than ever, in greater freedom. They are now taking the first few steps in a new world. Our future lies in their hands.

Epilogue

SO WHY ARE YOU STILL NOT CONVINCED?

We have fallen upon evil times
and the world has waxed very old and wicked.
Politics are very corrupt.
Children are no longer respectful to their parents.

> Inscription on a stone from Chaldea, 3800 BCE[1]

When you write a book with a positive message about the world, you are not exactly preaching to the choir. Ronald Bailey is an author who has done much to counter the perceptions of impending doom and disaster. When he presented his editor with a book proposal doing just that, the response he got sheds light on what people want to read: 'Ron, we'll publish this book and we'll both make some money. But I want to tell you that if you'd brought me a book predicting the end of the world, I could have made you a rich man.'[2]

It is fair to assume that people in general do not share the hopeful view of the world that I have presented in this book.

Fifty-four per cent of respondents in Britain, Australia, Canada and the United States rate the risk of our way of life ending within the next 100 years at fifty per cent or greater. Almost a quarter rated the risk of humans being wiped out at fifty per cent or greater.[3]

A couple of years ago, I commissioned a study in which 1,000 Swedes were asked eight questions about global development. Their lack of knowledge was stunning. On average, every age group and every income group were wrong on all eight questions. They thought that the world was bad and getting worse, and consistently underestimated the progress that had been made. Seventy-three per cent thought that hunger had increased and seventy-six per cent that extreme poverty had increased, during a period when they had both been reduced faster than at any other point in world history.[4] Those who had been through higher education actually had less knowledge of the progress that had been made against poverty and hunger, which makes you wonder how up-to-date their textbooks were.

The fact that this progress has bypassed most people has been confirmed by more recent studies. The Gapminder Foundation has done several 'ignorance' surveys using multiple-choice questions. In Britain, only ten per cent thought that world poverty had decreased in the last thirty years. More than half thought it had increased. In the United States, only five per cent answered correctly that world poverty had been almost halved in the last twenty years. Sixty-six per cent thought it had almost doubled.[5] Since they could also answer that poverty had remained the same, a random guess would have yielded a third correct answers, so the British performed significantly worse than a chimpanzee. Gapminder points out

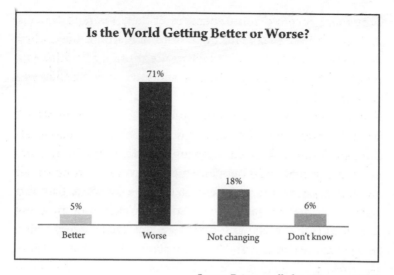

Is the World Getting Better or Worse?

71%

18%

5%

6%

Better   Worse   Not changing   Don't know

Source: Britons polled 8–9 January 2015,
YouGov/Human Zoo.

that we cannot call it ignorance if you can't beat a random choice; we must have inaccurate assumptions based on misleading or outdated information.

These assumptions are often formed by the media, which reinforces a particular way of looking at the world, a tendency to focus on the dramatic and surprising, which is almost always bad news, like war, murder and natural disasters. It seems that the more people watch TV news, the more they exaggerate the extent of crime. A study from Baltimore, where crime had been reduced quickly, showed that seventy-three per cent of those who watched the news every day were careful not to stay out too late in the city, compared to fifty-four per cent of those who watched it no more than twice a week. Almost everybody thought that crime was prevalent, but interestingly they always thought it occurred somewhere other than where they lived. Eighty-four per cent feared that criminals would harm their families, but as many as ninety-two per cent said they felt safe in their own neighbourhood. So the environment they had first-hand knowledge of felt safe, but the places they heard about on the news seemed very risky.[6]

Many journalists and editors acknowledge this tendency. The American public radio journalist Eric Weiner says: 'The truth is that unhappy people, living in profoundly unhappy places, make for good stories.'[7] When the Swedish TV journalist Freddie Ekman was asked about the biggest news stories during almost half a century in the trade, he responded by listing the murder of Prime Minister Olof Palme in 1986, the sinking of the cruise ferry *Estonia* in 1994, and the terror attacks of 9/11. When asked about any positive stories during this period, he answered, 'One doesn't remember them, because they never get big.'[8]

Ulrik Hagerup from Danish radio admits that journalists mostly report on 'the holes in the cheese' – problems and conflicts – but rarely about the cheese in itself – society and its progress. Mikael Österlund, a presenter on the Swedish radio news programme Ekot, explains that the most common reaction from listeners is, 'Why do you always describe the world as if it were impossible to live in it?' His answer is that it is their duty to talk about things that are wrong so people can decide whether that is how they want the world to be. It is also his job to describe deviations from what is expected – we expect aeroplanes to take off and land safely so we only report the crashes.[9]

From a broadcaster's perspective this makes sense. If a plane crashes we want to hear about it. But this also means that we shouldn't be content with getting our information from the news alone; we also need background and context, history and statistics. What is really impressive is the fact that forty million planes take off every year, and almost every one of them lands safely. Since the 1970s the number of passengers has increased more than ten-fold, and yet the number of accidents and fatalities has halved, but you would never know this from following the news.[10]

Max Roser, an economist at Oxford University who collects data on the world's development, puts it this way: 'Things that happen in an instant are mostly bad. It's this earthquake or that horrible murder. You're never going to have an article on the BBC or CNN that begins by saying: "There's no famine in south London today" or: "Child mortality again decreased by 0.005% in Botswana".'[11]

Journalists are always on the lookout for the most dramatic and shocking story from the geographic area they cover. There are many benefits to the kind of instant news that global TV networks and the internet have brought us. At last we have learned about the conditions under which people live in other parts of the world. But it also makes it easier for someone, somewhere to find something truly shocking to report on. There is always a war, and there is always a beastly child murderer on the loose, and that is what will top the news cycle – all the time. When we look at what is on the news as a whole, it gives us the impression that these are common occurrences, even increasingly common.

And of course, political parties, campaigners and pressure groups always exploit our fear to promote their own ideologies. The Ebola outbreak in West Africa in 2014–15 is an example of the collaboration between the media and organizations in scaring people. In September 2014 headlines screamed that 'US warns Ebola could infect 1.4 million by 2015' and 'CDC predicts as many as 1.4 million Ebola cases'. This came from a worst-case scenario calculated by the Center for Disease Control, which assumed speculatively that most cases were unreported and unknown, and assumed no interventions, and it was presented even in the abstract of the study as 'very unlikely'.[12] But it was the highest number and therefore the one that was picked up in the news and stuck in our minds.

In fact, every study had assumed that West Africans would just go on with risky behaviour as if nothing had happened. Other predictions seemed aimed at keeping Ebola in the news cycle. As the outbreak levelled off at 1,000 new cases per week in October 2014, the WHO warned there could be 5,000 to 10,000 per week by December. This turned into headlines like 'WHO expects 10,000 cases per week'. Total, worldwide cases resulting from the outbreak turned out to be around 30,000.

In a way, they were all doing their job. The institutions were trying to mobilize the world community with scary forecasts, and the media thought they had to warn us about the worst that could happen. But somewhere along the road they all forgot to remind us that this was 'highly unlikely', and the combined result was a completely distorted picture of the risks. Of course, this scare-mongering might have encouraged the very interventions that beat Ebola, but as the *Economist* points out, when authorities are constantly crying wolf, 'it will be harder to catch the world's attention next time.'[13]

As you read this, you might already have forgotten about Ebola and the fact that it never turned into the global nightmare we had anticipated. Perhaps you have turned your attention to the next worst-case scenario. An interesting experiment if you want a more realistic perspective on the world is to follow only local media. Since they only cover a very small geographical area it is more difficult for them to find horrible stories, which means that they give a more accurate description of what everyday life is like for most people. One summer I read *Strömstads Tidning*, a newspaper that covers a city with 6,000 inhabitants and its surroundings on the Swedish west coast. The stories were very different and much less dramatic than what I saw in national newspapers, on the BBC or on Twitter.

My favourite was a cover story with the title 'Everything was just fine'. It was about a driver who did not keep to the left when his car was being overtaken by another vehicle, so another driver thought that he had been drinking or taken drugs and called the police. They stopped him north of Strömstad. 'It turned out that the reported driver was sober and steady. Everything was just fine, says the policeman on duty.' Everything was actually just fine, and it was a common, everyday experience, but I bet that you have never read a story about it.[14]

The journalist Anders Bolling once asked a colleague why he never called criminologists to get a broader look at crime trends. 'It is so boring,' the colleague responded, 'because they only reply that crime is down.'[15] Bolling has concluded that it isn't constructive if people see the news as an accurate reflection of the world, since it usually gives us a tiny selection of the worst things that have happened in the last few hours. It is not that the individual stories are false, he points out, but that the combined effect functions as a distorted filter, which makes the world look worse and more dangerous than it is.

It would be easy to blame the media, but it is our own fault. If we didn't want to read about, listen to and watch bad news, journalists would not report it. Indeed, when they don't cover it, we often make up a worst-case scenario ourselves. When news reporters do not have access to a spectacular event, we often fill in the gaps with rumours and horror stories. When something bad happens anywhere, two billion smartphones will nowadays make sure that we find out, even if no reporters are on the scene.

The psychologists Daniel Kahneman and Amos Tversky have shown that people do not base their estimates of how frequent something is on data, but on how easy it is to recall examples from memory.[16] This 'availability heuristic' means that the more memorable an incident is, the more probable we think it is, so we imagine that horrible and shocking things, which stay in our thoughts, are more frequent than they are.

We are probably built to be worried. We are interested in exceptions. We notice the new things, the strange and unexpected. It's natural. We don't have to explain and understand normal, everyday things, but we do need to understand the exceptions. We don't tell our families about how we got home from work unless something really strange happened on the way.

We have been hardwired this way by evolution. Fear and worry are tools for survival. The hunters and gatherers who survived sudden storms and predators were the ones who had a tendency to scan the horizon for new threats rather than those who were relaxed and satisfied. In a more dangerous era, the cost of overreacting to a perceived threat was much smaller than the cost of underreacting. Those who were more worried and dissatisfied survived and spread their genes to us.

We are very interested in everything dangerous because people who weren't would have died by now. If the building is on fire, we need to know about it immediately. And even if the fire is only on television, it arouses some interest. Below layers of abstraction and desensitization, our stone-age brains produce some stress hormones and adrenaline when we sit there safely on the sofa, watching.

Steven Pinker mentions three psychological biases that make us think that the world is worse than it really is.[17] One is the well-documented fact that 'bad is stronger than good' – we are more likely to remember losing money, being abandoned by friends or receiving criticism than we are to remember winning money, gaining friends or receiving praise. The authors of a related study point out that 'negative information receives more processing and contributes more strongly to the final impression than does positive information.'[18]

Another emotional bias is the psychology of moralization. Complaining about problems is a way of sending a signal to others that you care about them, so critics are seen as more morally engaged. The seventeenth-century philosopher Thomas Hobbes also pointed out that criticizing the present was a way of competing with our rivals and contemporaries, whereas we can easily praise past generations, because they are not our competitors.

A third bias is our nostalgia about a golden age when life was supposedly simpler and better. The cultural historian Arthur Herman observed: 'Virtually every culture past or present has believed that men and women are not up to the standards of their parents and forebears.'[19] In the seventh century BCE, the poet Hesiod thought that there had once been a Golden Age when humans lived in harmony with the gods, and did not have to work since nature provided them with food. Then came a Silver Age with strife and worry, and a Bronze Age with even more strife and worry. Hesiod himself lived in the Iron Age, where conflict and immorality reined, where humans had to toil to survive. Most cultures, religions and ideologies have had similar mythologies relating a prehistorical lost paradise to which the decadent present is compared.

Many have sensed a connection between this idealization of the past with the idealization of our lost childhood, the nostalgic wish to return to a state of security and excitement. As we get older, we take on more responsibility, we sometimes get disillusioned or bored, and a certain decay of physical capacity sets it. It is easy to mistake changes in ourselves with changes in the times. Surprisingly often, when I ask people about their ideal era, the moment in world history that they think was the most harmonious and happy, they respond with the era they grew up in. Hence the nostalgia for the 1950s among the baby boomers. As grandpa Abe Simpson puts it in one episode of *The Simpsons*: 'I used to be with it, but then they changed what "it" was. Now, what I'm with isn't it, and what's "it" seems weird and scary to me.'

Enlightenment culture believed that progress was possible and that the world could steadily improve if human reason was set free, but even then, some thinkers like Rousseau and the Romantic philosophers thought that the world they had created was infinitely worse than what had existed before it. This has been a strong undercurrent in the Western world ever since, despite all the progress that has been achieved. It is still the reserve of every populist and demagogue today.

We constantly recreate our past and rearrange our memories, unconsciously. The two travellers Lasse Berg and Stig Karlsson realized that all their predictions of doom in Asia had been proven wrong, and that people's lives were getting better on a massive scale. But fascinatingly the people they visited did not always think so themselves. In the 1990s, the Indian woman Satto complained that life was now more difficult and she now had to work hard for her kids. Childhood had been much easier, she told them; she had just played all day.

'I thought about what interviews say and what they don't say,' Lasse Berg writes. 'If I had not been there before I would have drawn the obvious conclusion that a visiting journalist would after hearing that everything was getting worse.'[20] But Berg and Karlsson had actually been there two decades before and could compare what they now heard with their notes of what the villagers had said then about oppression, illiteracy and about how difficult it was for the family to get enough to eat. Satto did not play every day as she remembered – she worked hard in the fields every day.

When Berg returned again in 2010, Satto was happier with life and the living standard the family had attained, but fascinatingly, she claimed that she didn't remember her complaints during the 1990s visit. She now remembered that life was good in the 1990s as well.[21] It is never too late to have a happy childhood, apparently.

The fact that things have been getting better – overwhelmingly so – does not guarantee progress in the future. After years of easy money and debt financing of companies and governments, a large-scale financial crisis is possible, when all the bills are due. Global warming may threaten ecosystems and affect the lives of millions. Large-scale war between major powers is possible. Terrorists could wreak havoc on a massive scale if they get access to our most powerful technologies, but they could also co-ordinate a large number of smaller attacks on civilians. Most of all, people led by fear might curtail the freedom and the openness that progress depends on.

When Matt Ridley, author of *The Rational Optimist*, is asked what he is worried about he usually responds 'superstition and bureaucracy', because superstition can obstruct the accumulation of knowledge, and bureaucracy can stop us from applying that knowledge in new technologies and businesses.[22] Many of the achievements described in this book could still be obstructed by these forces. Radical Islamists stop girls from getting an education and try to reinstitute slavery where they get power. A false rumour, that the polio vaccine is a Western ploy to make Muslims infertile, has led to the return of polio, which was almost eradicated in several countries. Similarly, the nonsensical idea that the measles vaccine can cause autism has resulted in an anti-vaccination movement in the United States and several outbreaks of the horrible disease.

The causes of human progress are firmly entrenched – the growth of science and knowledge, the expansion of co-operation and trade, and the freedom to act on this. But historically this has been blocked and destroyed by forces that do not accept change, because they fear it or because it threatens their position. One thousand years ago, few would have guessed that Europe would be the place where the scientific and Industrial Revolution started. When Charlemagne was given an elaborate clock by the Caliph of Baghdad in 797, he did not understand what it was. At this time the Arabs were far ahead of Europe in science and technology, and kept Greek philosophy alive when it was all but forgotten in the West.

At the same time, the Song dynasty ruled over an economically and culturally flourishing China. The rule of law and a higher degree of economic freedom resulted in a climate of innovation. The Chinese used moveable type, gunpowder and the compass – the three inventions Francis Bacon saw as the most important for the world as late as 1620.

But the Ming dynasty, which took power in the fourteenth century, was hostile to technology and foreigners. It made oceanic navigation a capital offence and burned the great ships that might have discovered the world. Similarly, the Islamic world turned inwards after the Mongol invasions in the thirteenth century, purging many of the ideas of science and modernization. In the Ottoman Empire new technology was obstructed, the printing press was delayed for 300 years, and the modern Istanbul observatory of Taqi ad-Din built in 1577 was only allowed to stand for three years before it was destroyed for spying on God.

This is not to say that European powers knew any better. The élites also opposed new ideas and innovations, but the continent was too fractured – geographically, politically and linguistically – for any one group or emperor to control it all. In his book *The European Miracle*, the economic historian Eric Jones explains that in the fourteenth century there were 1,000 different political units in Europe, and in some ways this pluralism was still in place when we instituted a system of rival nation states.[23] New theories, inventions and business models could always survive somewhere, and prove their worth, until they were copied by others and won the day. Progress was always thrown a lifeline.

So it was not superior thinkers, inventors or businesses that made Europe rich, but the fact that European élites were less successful in obstructing them. Ideas, technology and capital could move between different states, which were forced to compete and learn from each other, and so push each other to modernization. This is somewhat similar to our era of globalization. More countries, in more places, now have access to the sum of humanity's knowledge, and are open to the best innovations from other places. In such a world, progress no longer depends on the whim of one emperor. If progress is blocked in one place, many others will continue humanity's journey.

Even though wealth and human lives can be destroyed, knowledge rarely disappears. It keeps on growing. Therefore any kind of backlash is unlikely to ruin human progress entirely. But progress is not automatic. All the progress that has been recorded in this book is the result of hard-working people, scientists, innovators and entrepreneurs with strange, new ideas, and brave individuals who fought for their freedom to do new things in new ways. If progress is to continue, you and I will have to carry the torch.

NOTES

Introduction: The good old days are now

1 Julian Simon, *The Ultimate Resource 2*. Princeton, NJ: Princeton University Press, 1996, p. 17.
2 Studio Ett, Swedish Public Radio, 2 February 2016.
3 Anders Bolling, *Apokalypsens gosiga mörker*. Stockholm: Bonniers, 2009, p. 15.
4 'Hearing to receive testimony on the impacts of sequestration and/or full-year continuing resolution of the Department of Defense', US Senate, Committee on Armed Services, Washington DC, 12 February 2013. http://www.armed-services.senate.gov/imo/media/doc/13-03%20-%202-12-13.pdf (accessed on 12 April 2016).
5 'Pope criticizes globalization, denies he is Marxist', *TeleSUR*, 11 January 2015. http://www.telesurtv.net/english/news/Pope-Criticizes-Globalization-Denies-he-is-Marxist-20150111-0015.html (accessed on 12 April 2016).
6 Suzanne Goldenberg, 'Naomi Klein: "We tried it your way and we don't have another decade to waste" ', *Guardian*, 14 September 2015, http://www.theguardian.com/books/2014/sep/14/naomi-klein-interview-capitalism-vs-the-climate (accessed on 12 April 2016).
7 John Gray, *Heresies: Against Progress and Other Illusions*. London: Granta UK, 2004, p. 32.
8 Angus Maddison, *The World Economy: Historical Statistics*. Paris: OECD, 2003, p. 262.

1 Food

1   Jonathan Swift, *Gulliver's Travels*. London: J. Walker, 1819, p. 148.
2   Christer Byström, 'Nödår', section in 'Sidensjös historia fore år 1900', http://web.comhem.se/chby/sidensjo/sidensjo.htm (accessed on 12 April 2016).
3   FAO, *The State of Food and Agriculture 1947*. Geneva: FAO, 1947; FAO, *Summary of Food and Agricultural Statistics 2003*. Rome: FAO, 2003; FAO, *The State of Food Insecurity in the World 2015*. Rome: FAO, 2015.
4   Fernand Braudel, *The Structures of Everyday Life: Civilization & Capitalism 15th–18th Century*, vol. 1. London: Phoenix Press, 2002, p. 73ff.
5   Braudel 2002, p. 78.
6   Braudel 2002, p. 78.
7   Braudel 2002, p. 77f.
8   Birgitta Conradson and Jane Fredlund, 'Köket förr i tiden: teknik i köket', www.ur.se/sundsvall/spring13a.html (accessed on 21 November 2002).
9   Gabriele Doblhammer and James W. Vaupel, 'Lifespan depends on month of birth', *Proceedings of the National Academy of Sciences of the United States*, 98, 5 (2001), 2934–9.
10 Braudel 2002, p. 74. Calories: Robert William Fogel, *The Escape From Hunger and Premature Death, 1700–2100: Europe, America, and the Third World*. Cambridge: Cambridge University Press, 2004, p. 9.
11 Angus Deaton, *The Great Escape: Health, Wealth and the Origins of Inequality*. Princeton, NJ: Princeton University Press, 2013, p. 92.
12 Fogel 2004, p. 33.
13 Matt Ridley, *The Rational Optimist: How Prosperity Evolves*. London: Fourth Estate, 2010, p. 6f.
14 Max Roser, 'Food per person' (2015), *OurWorldInData.org*, http://ourworldindata.org/data/food-agriculture/food-per-person/ (accessed on 21 March 2016).
15 Rebecca Onion, 'A post-World War I "Hunger Map of Europe," aimed at the hearts of American kids', *The Vault, Slate*, 31 July 2014, http://www.slate.com/blogs/the_vault/2014/07/31/history_of_famine_in_europe_after_wwi_a_hunger_map_for_american_kids.html (accessed on 21 March 2016).

NOTES

16 United States Food Administration, *Food Saving and Sharing*. Washington DC: Govt. Printing Office, 1918, pp. ii, 92.

17 Vaclav Smil, *Enriching the Earth: Fritz Haber, Carl Bosch, and the Transformation of World Food Production*. Cambridge, MA: MIT Press, 2004, p. xiii.

18 Peter Herrlich, 'The responsibility of the scientist', *EMBO Reports*, 14, 9 (September 2013), 758–64.

19 Torbjörn Fagerström, 'Den värdefulla rätten att mjölka en kossa', *Dagens Nyheter*, 18 March 2013.

20 Fogel 2004, p. 90.

21 Deaton 2013, p. 158.

22 Max Roser, 'Fertility rates' (2015), *OurWorldInData.org*, http://ourworldindata.org/data/population-growth-vital-statistics/fertility-rates/ (accessed on 21 March 2016).

23 Paul Ehrlich, *The Population Bomb*. New York: Ballantine Books, p. 11.

24 William and Paul Paddock, *Famine 1975*. Boston: Little, Brown & Co, 1968, p. 8.

25 Much of the following is based on Gregg Easterbrook, 'Forgotten benefactor of humanity', *Atlantic*, 270, 1 (1997), 75–82.

26 'Crops supply per person per day', *Human Progress*, http://humanprogress.org/f1/2126 (accessed on 21 March 2016); 'World agricultural price (Grilli-Yang) index', *Human Progress*, http://humanprogress.org/static/3020 (accessed on 21 March 2016).

27 FAO 1947.

28 J. L. van Zanden et al. (eds), *How Was Life? Global Well-Being since 1820*. OECD Publishing, 2014, doi: 10.1787/9789264214262-en, chap. 7.

29 K. von Grebmer, J. Bernstein, A. de Waal, N. Prasai, S. Yin and Y. Yohannes, *2015 Global Hunger Index: Armed Conflict and the Challenge of Hunger*. Bonn, Washington, DC, and Dublin: Welthungerhilfe, International Food Policy Research Institute, and Concern Worldwide, 2015.

30 Bjorn Lomborg (ed.), *How Much have Global Problems Cost the World?: A Scorecard from 1900 to 2050*. Cambridge: Cambridge University Press, 2013.

31 Jesse Ausubel, 'Peak farmland', lecture for the Symposium in Honor of Paul Demeny, New York, 16 December 2012.

32 Quoted in Jim Prevor, 'Feeding the world in 2050', *American Food and Ag Exporter* (Fall 2009), 10–14, p. 14.

33 Easterbrook 1997.
34 'Total fertility', United Nations Population Division, downloaded 31 October 2015. United Nations, Department of Economic and Social Affairs, Population Division, 'World Fertility Patterns 2015 – Data Booklet' (ST/ESA/ SER.A/370) (2015).
35 Von Grebmer et al. 2015.
36 Jang Jin-sung, *Dear Leader: My Escape from North Korea*. New York: Simon & Schuster, 2015, p. 237f.
37 Von Grebmer et al. 2015.
38 Amartya Sen, *Development as Freedom*. New York: Anchor Books, 1999, chap. 7.
39 Kate Xiao Zhou, *How the Farmers Changed China: Power of the People*. Boulder, CO: Westview Press, 1996, p. 56.
40 'Xiaogang Village, birthplace of rural reform, moves on', *China Development Gateway*, 16 December 2008, http://en.chinagate.cn/ features/rural_poverty/2008-12/16/content_16966805.htm (accessed on 21 March 2016).

2 Sanitation

1   G. K. Chesterton, *The Man Who Was Thursday*. New York: Barnes & Noble, 2004, p. 5.
2   Ann Lindstrand, Staffan Bergström, Hans Rosling, Birgitta Rubenson, Bo Stenson and Thorild Tylleskär, *Global Health: An Introductory Textbook*. Lund: Studentlitteratur, 2006, p. 77.
3   WHO, *The World Health Report 1995: Bridging the Future*. Geneva: WHO, 1995; WHO and UNICEF, *Progress on Sanitation and Drinking Water: 2015 Update and MDG Assessment*. Geneva: WHO and UNICEF, 2015.
4   Quoted in Rose George, *The Big Necessity: Adventures in the World of Human Waste*. London: Portobello, paperback edition, 2009, p. 86.
5   Claire Tomalin, *Samuel Pepys: The Unequalled Self*. London: Penguin Books, 2003, p. 5.
6   Otto L. Bettman, *The Good Old Days: They Were Terrible*. New York: Random House, 1974, p. 35.
7   Bill Emmott, *20/21 Vision: The Lessons of the 20th Century for the 21st*. London: Penguin, 2004, p. 257f.

8   Per-Anders Fogelström, *Ladugårdslandet som blev Östermalm*. Stockholm: Billbergs, 1964, p. 18.

9   Deaton 2013, p. 95.

10   First Reading, HC Deb 15 July 1858 vol. 151 cc1508–40, http://hansard.millbanksystems.com/commons/1858/jul/15/first-reading#S3V0151P0_18580715_HOC_123 (accessed on 21 March 2016).

11   David Cutler and Grant Miller, 'The role of public health improvements in health advances: the 20th century United States', Working Paper 10511, National Bureau of Economic Research, May 2004.

12   WHO and UNICEF 2015. The 1980 number is from WHO 1995.

13   Fredrik Segerfeldt, *Water for Sale: How Business and the Market Can Resolve the World's Water Crisis*. Washington DC: Cato Institute, 2005, p. 13f.

14   UNDP, *Human Development Report 2006: Beyond Scarcity: Power, Poverty and the Global Water Crisis*. New York: UNDP, 2006, p. 14.

15   UNDP 2006, p. 47.

16   Adelaide Lusambili, ' "It is our dirty little secret": an ethnographic study of the flying toilets in Kibera Slums, Nairobi', STEPS Working Paper 44. Brighton: STEPS Centre, 2011, p. 12.

17   WHO and UNICEF 2015.

3 Life expectancy

1   M. C. Buer, *Health, Wealth and Population in the Early Days of the Industrial Revolution*. Abingdon: Routledge, 2013, p. 88.

2   Rosemay Horrox, *The Black Death*. Manchester: Manchester University Press, 1994, p. 65.

3   Horrox 1994, p. 82ff.

4   Max Roser, 'Life expectancy' (2016), *OurWorldInData.org*, http://ourworldindata.org/data/population-growth-vital-statistics/life-expectancy/ (accessed on 21 March 2016).

5   Braudel 2002, p. 85.

6   Deaton 2013, p. 77.

7   Abdel R. Omran, 'The epidemiologic transition: a theory of the epidemiology of population change', *Milbank Quarterly*, 83, 4 (2005), 731–57.

8   Oskar Burgera, Annette Baudischa and James W. Vaupel, 'Human mortality improvement in evolutionary context', *Proceedings of the National Academy of Sciences of the United States of America*, 109, 44 (2012), 18210–14.

9   Max Roser, 'Child mortality' (2015), *OurWorldInData.org*, http://ourworldindata.org/data/population-growth-vital-statistics/child-mortality/ (accessed on 21 March 2016).

10   Fogel 2004, p. 110f.

11   Omran 2005.

12   Deaton 2013, p. 84f.

13   Max Roser, 'Maternal mortality' (2015), *OurWorldInData.org*, http://ourworldindata.org/data/health/maternal-mortality/ (accessed on 21 March 2015); World Bank, 'World Development Indicators 2015', 1 December 2015, http://data.worldbank.org/data-catalog/world-development-indicators (accessed on 12 April 2015).

14   Carlo A. Corsini and Pier Paolo Viazzo (eds), *The Decline of Infant Mortality in Europe 1800–1950: Four National Case Studies*. Florence: UNICEF, 1993.

15   Charles Kenny, *Getting Better, Why Global Development Is Succeeding – and How We Can Improve the World Even More*. New York: Basic Books, 2012, p. 12.

16   WHO, *The Global Eradication of Smallpox: Final Report of the Global Commission for the Certification of Smallpox Eradication*. Geneva: WHO, 1980.

17   WHO, *World Malaria Report 2015*. Geneva: WHO, 2015.

18   Deaton 2013, p. 151.

19   UNAIDS, 'Fact Sheet 2015', 2015, http://www.unaids.org/sites/default/files/media_asset/20150901_FactSheet_2015_en.pdf (accessed on 12 April 2016); Deaton 2013, p. 151.

20   World Bank, 'World Development Indicators 2015'.

21   World Bank, 'World Development Indicators 2015'; United Nations, *The Millennium Development Goals Report*. New York: United Nations, 2015, p. 5.

22   Joshua Nalibow Ruxin, 'Magic bullet: the history of oral rehydration therapy', *Medical History*, 38 (1994), 363–97.

23   David E. Bloom, '7 billion and counting', *Science*, 333 (2011), 562–9.

24   Kenny 2012, chap. 6.

25   William Easterly, 'Life during growth', *Journal of Economic Growth*, 4, 3 (1999), 239–76.

26 Ronald Bailey, *The End of Doom: Environmental Renewal in the Twenty-First Century*. New York: St Martin's Press, 2015, chap. 4; 'More than 1.5 million cancer deaths averted in last two decades', *CBS News*, 31 December 2014, http://www.cbsnews.com/news/more-than-1-million-cancer-deaths-averted-in-last-two-decades (accessed on 21 March 2016).

27 World Bank, 'World Development Indicators 2015'.

28 In 2013 it was 86.6 years.

29 Jim Oeppen and James W. Vaupel, 'Broken limits to life expectancy', *Science*, 296, 5579 (2002), 1029–31.

30 Deaton 2013, p. 149.

4 Poverty

1 Jane Jacobs, *The Economy of Cities*. New York: Random House, 1969, p. 121.

2 Braudel 2002, p. 283.

3 Maddison 2003, p. 262.

4 Francois Bourguignon and Christian Morrisson, 'Inequality among world citizens: 1820–1992', *American Economic Review*, 92, 4 (2002), 727–44; World Bank, *PovcalNet*, http://iresearch.worldbank.org/PovcalNet; Marcio Cruz, James Foster, Bryce Quillin and Philip Schellekens, 'Ending extreme poverty and sharing prosperity: progress and policies', Policy Research Note no. 3, October 2015.

5 Martin Ravallion, 'Poverty in the rich world when it was not nearly so rich' (2014), blog post, Center for Global Development, Washington DC, http://www.cgdev.org/blog/poverty-rich-world-when-it-was-not-nearly-so-rich (accessed on 12 April 2016).

6 Fogel 2004, p. 41.

7 Adam Smith, *An Inquiry Into the Nature and Causes of the Wealth of Nations*, Glasgow Edition of the Works and Correspondence of Adam Smith. Indianapolis: Liberty Fund, 1981, bk. 1, ch. 8.

8 Peter Lindert and Jeffrey Williamson, 'English workers' living standards during the Industrial Revolution: a new look', in Joel Mokyr (ed.), *The Economics of the Industrial Revolution*. London: Allen & Unwin, 1985.

9 Fogel 2004, p. 38.

10   World Bank, *World Development Report 1997: The State in a Changing World*. Washington DC: World Bank Group, 1997.

11   Lasse Berg, *Ut ur Kalahari: Drömmen om det goda livet*. Stockholm: Ordfront, 2014, p. 63.

12   Berg 2014, p. 60. Their first return visit is described in Lasse Berg and Stig Karlsson, *I Asiens tid: Indien, Kina, Japan*. Stockholm: Ordfront, 2000.

13   Swaminathan S. Anklesaria Aiyar, 'Capitalism's assault on the Indian caste system', *Cato Policy Analysis*, 776, 21 July 2015, p. 12.

14   World Bank, 'Voices of the poor', http://web.worldbank.org/WBSITE/EXTERNAL/TOPICS/EXTPOVERTY/0,,contentMDK:20622514~menuPK:336998~pagePK:148956~piPK:216618~theSitePK:336992,00.html (accessed on 16 April 2016), p. 41.

15   'What the poor say', Washington DC: World Bank Group, May 2001, http://siteresources.worldbank.org/INTPOVERTY/Resources/poor.pdf (accessed on 12 April 2016).

16   Lant Pritchett, 'Divergence, big time', *Journal of Economic Perspectives*, 11, 3 (1997), 3–17, p. 3.

17   Arvind Subramanian and Martin Kessler, 'The hyperglobalization of trade and its future', Working Paper 3, Global Citizen Foundation, 2013.

18   Peter Hartcher, 'Tipping point from West to rest just passed', *Sydney Morning Herald*, 17 April 2012.

19   Bourguignon and Morrisson 2002.

20   John Rawls, *A Theory of Justice*. Oxford: Oxford University Press, 1973; see application of this in Bjørn Lomborg, *The Skeptical Environmentalist: Measuring the Real State of the World*. Cambridge: Cambridge University Press, 2001, p. 64.

21   Max Roser, 'World poverty' (2016), *OurWorldInData.org*, http://ourworldindata.org/data/growth-and-distribution-of-prosperity/world-poverty/ (accessed on 21 March 2016).

22   David Dollar, Tatjana Kleineberg and Aart Kraay, 'Growth still is good for the poor', Working Paper 596, Luxembourg Income Study, Cross-National Data Center in Luxembourg, 2013, p. 17.

23   UN-HABITAT, *State of the World's Cities 2012/13: Prosperity of Cities*. Nairobi: UN-HABITAT, 2012, p. 126; United Nations, The Millennium Development Goals Report 2015, p. 60.

24   World Bank, *A Measured Approach to Ending Poverty and Boosting Shared Prosperity: Concepts, Data, and the Twin Goals*. Washington, DC: World Bank Group, 2015, p. 44ff.

25   Tomáš Hellebrandt and Paolo Mauro, 'The future of worldwide income distribution', Working Paper 15-7, Peterson Institute for International Economics, 2015.

5 Violence

1   Henry Maine, *International Law: A Series of Lectures Delivered Before the University of Cambridge*. H. Holt, 1887, p. 8.

2   Steven Pinker, *The Better Angels of Our Nature: The Decline of Violence in History and Its Causes*. London: Allen Lane, 2011, p. xxi.

3   P. Davies, L. Lee, A. Fox and E. Fox, 'Could nursery rhymes cause violent behaviour: a comparison with television viewing', *Archives of Diseases in Childhood*, 89 (2004), 1103–5.

4   Manuel Eisner, 'Long-term historical trends in violent crime', *Crime and Justice*, 30 (2003), 83–142.

5   Pinker 2011, p. 132.

6   Pinker 2011, p. 52f.

7   Eisner 2003.

8   Barbara Tuchman, *A Distant Mirror: The Calamitous 14th Century*. New York: Random House, 2011, p. 135.

9   Eisner 2003.

10 Jan Philipp Reemtsma, *Trust and Violence: An Essay on a Modern Relationship*. Princeton, NJ: Princeton University Press, 2012, p. 118.

11 Pinker 2011, p. 81.

12 Pinker 2011, p. 159.

13 Matthew White, *The Great Big Book of Horrible Things: The Definitive Chronicle of History's 100 Worst Atrocities*. New York: W. W. Norton & Company, p. 93.

14 Peter Brecke, 'Conflict catalog (violent conflicts 1400 AD to the present in different regions of the world)', http://www.cgeh.nl/data#conflict (accessed on 15 April 2016).

15 Pinker 2011, p. 231.

16 Pinker 2011, p. 232.

17 C. V. Wedgwood, *The Thirty Years' War*. New York: New York Review Books Classic, 2005, p. 14f.

18 John Mueller, *Retreat from Doomsday: The Obsolescence of Major War*. New York: Basic Books, 2001, p. 18.

19   Pinker 2011, p. 224ff.
20   Mueller 2001, p. 5.
21   Max Roser, 'War and Peace after 1945'(2015), *OurWorldInData.org*, http://ourworldindata.org/data/war-peace/war-and-peace-after-1945/ (accessed on 22 March 2016).
22   *Human Security Report 2005*. New York: Oxford University Press, 2005, p. 75.
23   Frank Chalk and Kurt Jonassohn, *The History and Sociology of Genocide: Analyses and Case Studies*. New Haven: Yale University Press, 1990, pp. xvii, 58.
24   *Human Security Report 2013*. Vancouver: Human Security Press, 2014.
25   WHO, 'European Detailed Mortality Database', http://data.euro.who.int/dmdb/ (accessed on 22 March 2016).
26   Audrey Cronin, *How Terrorism Ends: Understanding the Decline and Demise of Terrorist Campaigns*. Princeton, NJ: Princeton University Press, 2009, p. 114.
27   Norman Angell, *The Great Illusion*. New York: Cosimo Classics, 2007.
28   Bruce M. Russett and John R. Oneal, *Triangulating Peace: Democracy, Interdependence, and International Organizations*. New York: W. W. Norton & Company, 2001; Ludwig von Mises, *Human Action: A Treatise on Economics*, 3rd revised edition. Chicago: Contemporary Books, 1966, section 6.XXXIV.29.

6 The environment

1   'Indira Gandhi's address', *The Times of India*, 15 June 1972.
2   John Nielsen, 'The killer fog of '52', NPR, 11 December 2002, http://www.npr.org/templates/story/story.php?storyId=873954 (accessed on 22 March 2016).
3   Michelle L. Bell, Devra L. Davis and Tony Fletcher, 'A retrospective assessment of mortality from the London smog episode of 1952: the role of influenza and pollution'. *Environmental Health Perspectives*. 2004 January; 112(1): 6–8.
4   Department for Environment, Food and Rural Affairs, 'Emissions of air pollutants in the UK, 1970–2013', 18 December 2014.
5   Donella H. Meadows, Dennis L. Meadows, Jørgen Randers and William W. Behrens III, *The Limits to Growth*. Washington DC: Potomac Associates, 1972, p. 71.

NOTES

6 United States Environmental Protection Agency, 'Air quality trends', http://www3.epa.gov/airtrends/aqtrends.html (accessed on 22 March 2016); Department for Environment, Food and Rural Affairs 2014.

7 Department for Environment, Food and Rural Affairs 2014.

8 Lomborg 2001, p. 164f.

9 Mattias Svensson, *Miljöpolitik för moderater*. Stockholm: Fores, 2015, p. 26.

10 International Tanker Owners Pollution Federation Limited, 'Oil tanker spill statistics 2014' (2015), http://www.itopf.com/fileadmin/data/Documents/Company_Lit/Oil_Spill_Stats_2014FINALlowres.pdf (accessed on 12 April 2016).

11 European Environment Agency, 'Exposure of ecosystems to acidification, eutrophication and ozone', 27 November 2015, http://www.eea.europa.eu/data-and-maps/indicators/exposure-of-ecosystems-to-acidification-3/assessment-1 (accessed on 22 March 2016).

12 Forest Europe, *State of Europe's Forests 2015*. Madrid: Ministerial Conference on the Protection of Forests in Europe, 2015; FAO, *Global Forest Resource Assessment 2015*. Rome: FAO, 2015; Brad Plumer, 'Brazil's recent fight against deforestation has been a huge success', *Vox*, 14 June 2015.

13 Ausubel 2012, p. 2.

14 Bailey 2015, chap. 7.

15 Maria Dornelas, Nicholas J. Gotelli, Brian McGill, Hideyasu Shimadzu, Faye Moyes, Caya Sievers and Anne E. Magurran, 'Assemblage time series reveal biodiversity change but not systematic loss', *Science*, 344.6181, 18 April 2014, pp. 296, 298.

16 The index was developed by Yale Center for Environmental Law and Policy and Center for International Earth Science Information Network at Columbia University.

17 A. Hsu, J. Emerson, M. Levy, A. de Sherbinin, L. Johnson, O. Malik, J. Schwartz and M. Jaiteh, *The 2014 Environmental Performance Index*. New Haven, CT: Yale Center for Environmental Law & Policy, 2014.

18 Lance A. Ealey and Glenn A. Mercer, 'Tomorrow's cars, today's engines', *McKinsey Quarterly*, 3 (2002).

19 Bailey 2015, p. 115f.

20 Bailey 2015, chap. 4.

21 US Geological Survey, *Mineral Commodity Summaries 2015*. Washington DC: US Geological Survey, 2015, http://dx.doi.org/10.3133/70140094, p. 191.

22 Blake Clayton, *Market Madness: A Century of Oil Panics, Crises, and Crashes*. Oxford: Oxford University Press, 2015, p. 17f.

23 Environmental Performance Index 2006.

24 Indur M. Goklany, *The Improving State of the World: Why We're Living Longer, Healthier, More Comfortable Lives on a Cleaner Planet*. Washington, DC: Cato Institute, 2007, p. 149f.

25 Bishwa S. Koirala, Hui Li and Robert P. Berrens, 'Further investigation of environmental Kuznets curve studies using meta-analysis', *International Journal of Ecological Economics and Statistics*, 22, S11 (2011).

26 Indur Goklany, 'Deaths and death rates from extreme weather events: 1900–2008'. *Journal of American Physicians and Surgeons*, 14, 4 (2009), 102–9.

27 Todd Moss and Benjamin Leo, 'Maximizing access to energy: estimates of access and generation for the overseas private investment corporation's portfolio', Center for Global Development, January 2014, www.cgdev.org/publication/maximizing-access-energy-estimates-access-and-generation-overseas-private-investment (accessed on 22 March 2016).

28 Bailey 2015, p. 200.

29 Lindstrand et al. 2006, p. 70. In fact, infant mortality in Bosnia and Croatia fell by around one fourth during the war years.

30 Goklany 2009.

31 Peter H. Diamandis and Steven Kotler, *Abundance: The Future is Better Than You Think*. New York: Free Press, 2012, p. 169.

7 Literacy

1 Plutarch, *On Listening to Lectures*, 46 BC, Section 18.

2 Berg 2014, p. 80.

3 OECD, 'World development of literacy and attainment of at least basic education, 1820–2010', statistical appendix to van Zanden et al. 2014, http://dx.doi.org/10.1787/888933095666 (accessed on 21 February 2016).

4 van Zanden et al. 2014, chap. 5. For a history, see UNESCO, *Literacy for Life, Global Monitoring Report 2006*. Paris: UNESCO, 2005, chap. 8.

5 Derek Gillard, 'Education in England: a brief history' (2011), http://www.educationengland.org.uk/history/chapter03 (accessed on 22 March 2016).

6 Erik Lidström, *Education Unchained: What It Takes to Restore Schools and Learning*. Lanham, MD: Rowman & Littlefield, 2015, p. 63.

7 van Zanden et al. 2014.

8 van Zanden et al. 2014. The 2015 estimate is from UNESCO, 'Education for All 2000–2015: Achievements and Challenges', EFA Global Monitoring Report 2015. Paris: UNESCO, 2015.

9 Kenny 2012, p. 80.

10 United Nations 2015.

11 Kenny 2012, p. 81.

12 United Nations 2015.

13 Kenny 2012, p. 79; United Nations 2015.

14 UNESCO 2005, p. 196f.

15 'Learning unleashed', *The Economist*, August 1, 2015.

16 Ibid.

17 James Tooley, *The Beautiful Tree: A Personal Journey into How the World's Poorest People Are Educating Themselves*. Washington DC: Cato Institute, 2009, pp. 174, 258–9.

18 World Bank, 'World Development Indicators 2015', exc. 1970.

19 United Nations 2015.

20 Frederick Douglass, *The Life and Times of Frederick Douglass*. North Chelmsford, MA: Courier Corporation, 2012, p. 141.

21 Douglass 2012, chap. 7.

8 Freedom

1 Voltaire, *L'Ingénu*, 1767, chap. 10.

2 Douglass 2012, chap. 7.

3 Robert Guest, *The Shackled Continent*. London: Pan Books 2005, p. 8.

4 Paul Petit, *Pax Romana*. Berkeley and Los Angeles: University of California Press, 1976, p. 162.

5 Michael Shermer, *The Moral Arc: How Science and Reason Lead Humanity Toward Truth, Justice, and Freedom*. New York: Henry Holt and Company, 2015, p. 194.

6   Shermer 2015, p. 206.

7   Shermer 2015, pp. 205f.

8   *The Papers of Thomas Jefferson*, vol. 1, 1760–1776. Ed. Julian P. Boyd. Princeton: Princeton University Press, 1950, p. 243ff.

9   General Treaty, signed in Congress, at Vienna, 9 June 1815, Act XV: 'Declaration of the powers, on the abolition of the slave trade, of the 8th February 1815', Wikisource: https://en.wikisource.org/wiki/Final_Act_of_the_Congress_of_Vienna/Act_XV (accessed on 12 April 2016).

10 Alexander Stephens, Cornerstone Speech, 21 March 1861. Wikisource: https://en.wikisource.org/wiki/Cornerstone_Speech (accessed on 12 April 2016).

11 Manisha Sinha, *The Counterrevolution of Slavery: Politics and Ideology in Antebellum South Carolina*. Chapel Hill: University of North Carolina Press, 2000, p. 255f.

12 Shermer 2015, p. 211.

13 John Mueller, *Capitalism, Democracy, and Ralph's Pretty Good Grocery*. Princeton, NJ: Princeton University Press, 2001, p. 214.

14 Freedom House, 'Number and percentages of electoral democracies, FIW 1989–2015', https://freedomhouse.org/sites/default/files/Number%20and%20Percentage%20of%20Electoral%20Democracy%2C%20FIW%201989-2015.pdf (accessed on 22 March 2016).

15 Adam Przeworski, Michael E. Alvarez, Jose Antonio Cheibub and Fernando Limongi, *Democracy and Development: Political Institutions and Well-Being in the World, 1950–1990*. Cambridge: Cambridge University Press, 2000, p. 88.

16 Przeworski et al. 2000.

17 Pew Research Center, 'The world's Muslims: religion, politics and society: survey topline results'. Washington DC: Pew Research Center's Forum on Religion & Public Life, 2013.

18 Freedom House, 'Global country status overview, FIW 1973–2015', https://freedomhouse.org/sites/default/files/Global%20Country%20Status%20Overview%2C%201973-2015.pdf (accessed on 22 March 2016).

19 Freedom House, 'Freedom of the press 2015'. Washington DC: Freedom House, 2015, p. 8.

20 James Gwartney, Robert Lawson and Joshua Hall, *Economic Freedom of the World: 2015 Annual Report*. Vancouver: Fraser Institute, 2015.

21 Milton Friedman, 'Economic freedom, human freedom, political freedom' (1991), in Micheline Ishay (ed.), *The Human Rights Reader: Major Political Essays, Speeches, and Documents from Ancient Times to the Present*. Taylor & Francis, 2007, p. 346.

22 Freedom House, 'Freedom in the world 2015'. Washington DC: Freedom House, 2015.

9 Equality

1 Charles Darwin, *The Descent of Man, and Selection in Relation to Sex*. Princeton, NJ: Princeton University Press, 2008, part 1, p. 100.

2 Pinker 2011, p. 658.

3 Shermer 2015, p. 18.

4 John Locke, *A Letter Concerning Toleration*. Peterborough, ON: Broadview Press, 2013, p. 85.

5 James R. Flynn, *What is Intelligence? Beyond the Flynn Effect*. Cambridge: Cambridge University Press, 1st expanded pbk edn, 2009, p. 18f.

6 Pinker 2011, p. 656.

7 Karl Marx and Friedrich Engels, 'Manifesto of the Communist Party', in Karl Marx and Friedrich Engels, *Basic Writings on Politics and Philosophy*. London: Fontana, 1984, p. 52.

8 Benjamin M. Friedman, *The Moral Consequences of Growth*. New York: Alfred A Knopf, 2005.

9 Ronald Inglehart, *Modernization and Postmodernization: Cultural, Economic and Political Change in 43 Societies*. Princeton, NJ: Princeton University Press, 1997, p. 40.

10 Brink Lindsey, *The Age of Abundance: How Prosperity Transformed America's Politics and Culture*. New York: Collins, 2007, p. 104.

11 Abigail Thernstrom and Stephan Thernstrom, *America in Black and White: One Nation, Indivisible*. New York: Simon & Schuster, Touchstone edition, 1999, p. 31.

12 Pinker 2011, p. 390f.

13 'Trends in American values 1987–2012', The Pew Research Center, 4 June 2012.

14 Victor Asal and Amy Pate, 'The decline of ethnic political discrimination, 1950–2003', in Monty G. Marshall and Ted Robert Gurr (eds),

Peace and Conflict 2005. College Park, MD: Center for International Development & Conflict Management, University of Maryland, 2005, p. 38.

15 Margo Wilson and Martin Daly, 'The man who mistook his wife for a chattel', in J. H. Barkow, L. Cosmides and J. Tooby (eds), *The Adapted Mind. Evolutionary Psychology and the Generation of Culture*. New York: Oxford University Press, 1992.

16 Mary Wollstonecraft, *A Vindication of the Rights of Woman*, 3rd edition. London: J. Johnson, 1796, p. 90.

17 'Bolting among the ladies', *Oneida Whig*, 1 August 1848.

18 Nicola Lacey, Celia Wells and Oliver Quick, *Reconstructing Criminal Law: Text and Materials*. Cambridge: Cambridge University Press, 2003, p. 488.

19 World Economic Forum, 'Global gender gap report 2015', http://www.weforum.org/reports/global-gender-gap-report-2015 (accessed on 22 March 2016).

20 UNDP, *Human Development Report 2014*. New York: UNDP, 2014.

21 Pinker 2011, p. 413.

22 United Nations Children's Fund, *Female Genital Mutilation/Cutting: What Might the Future Hold?* New York: UNICEF, 2014.

23 Pew Research Center 2013.

24 Jean M. Twenge, 'Attitudes toward women, 1970–1995: a meta-analysis', *Psychology of Women Quarterly*, 21, 1 (1997), 35–51.

25 Pinker 2011, p. 408f.

26 Lillian Faderman, *The Gay Revolution: The Story of the Struggle*. New York: Simon and Schuster, 2015, p. 137.

27 Aaron Day: 'The PinkNews guide to the history of England and Wales equal marriage', *PinkNews*, 15 July 2013.

28 John D'Emilio, *Sexual Politics, Sexual Communities*, 2nd edn. Chicago: University of Chicago Press, 2012, p. 156.

29 Faderman 2015.

30 'The gay divide', *The Economist*, 11 October 2014.

10 The next generation

1 Julian L. Simon (ed.), *The State of Humanity*. Oxford and Cambridge: Blackwell, 1995, p. 27.

NOTES

2 Eli F. Heckscher, *Industrialismen: Den ekonomiska utvecklingen sedan 1750*, 4th edition. Stockholm: Kooperativa Förbundets Bokförlag, 1948, p. 115.

3 ILO, *Economically Active Populations: Estimates and Projections, 1950–2010*. Geneva: ILO, 1996; ILO, *Marking Progress Against Child Labour: Global Estimates and Trends 2000–2012*. Geneva: ILO, 2013.

4 Martin Ravaillon, *Economics of Poverty: History, Measurement and Policy*. New York: Oxford University Press, 2016.

5 UNICEF, *Child Labour in Historical Perspective 1800–1985: Case Studies from Europe, Japan and Colombia*. Ed. Hugh Cunningham and Pier Paolo Viazzo. Florence: UNICEF, 1996, p. 41.

6 Kaushik Basu, 'Child labor: cause, consequence and cure, with remarks on international labor standards', *Journal of Economic Literature*, 37, 3 (1999), 1083–19.

7 Clark Nardinelli, *Child Labor and the Industrial Revolution*. Bloomington: Indiana University Press, 1990, p. 115.

8 ILO, UNICEF, and World Bank, 'Understanding children's work in Vietnam: report on child labour', April 2009, http://www.ucw-project.org/attachment/child_labour_Vietnam20110627_125424.pdf (accessed on 12 April 2016).

9 Eric V. Edmonds and Norbert Schady, 'Poverty alleviation and child labor', Working Paper 15345, National Bureau of Economic Research, 2009.

10 Eric Edmonds and Nina Pavcnik, 'Child labor in the global economy', *Journal of Economic Perspectives*, 19, 1 (2005), 199–220; Eric Edmonds, Nina Pavcnik and Petia Topalova, 'Trade adjustment and human capital investments: evidence from Indian tariff reform'. Working Paper 12884, National Bureau of Economic Research, 2007.

11 ILO 1996.

12 ILO 2013.

13 UNICEF 1996, p. 52.

14 Ronald Inglehart, Roberto Foa, Christopher Peterson and Christian Welzel, 'Development, freedom, and rising happiness: a global perspective (1981–2007)', *Association for Psychological Science*, 3, 4 (2008), 264–85, p. 264.

15 Herbert Spencer, 'The Kantian idea of rights', appendix 1 in *The Principles of Ethics*, vol. II. Indianapolis: Liberty Fund, 1978.

16 Berg and Karlsson 2000, p. 42.

Epilogue: So why are you still not convinced?

1 George Thomas White Patrick, 'The new optimism', *Popular Science Monthly* (May 1913), p. 493.

2 Bailey 2015, p. xvii.

3 Melanie Randle and Richard Eckersley, 'Public perceptions of future threats to humanity and different societal responses: a cross-national study', *Futures*, 72 (2015), 4–16.

4 Johan Norberg, 'Rubriker som gör oss rädda'. Timbro, 2005.

5 Hans Rosling, 'Highlights from Ignorance Survey in the UK', 3 November 2013, http://www.gapminder.org/news/highlights-from-ignorance-survey-in-the-uk (accessed on 22 March 2016); Gapminder, 'The Ignorance Survey: United States', 2013, http://www.gapminder.org/GapminderMedia/wp-uploads/Results-from-the-Ignorance-Survey-in-the-US.pdf (accessed on 12 April 2016).

6 Mark Crispin Miller, 'It's a crime: the economic impact of the local TV news'. New York: Project on Media Ownership, 1998.

7 Eric Weiner, *The Geography of Bliss: One Grump's Search for the Happiest Places in the World*. New York: Twelve, 2008, p. 1f.

8 'De roliga nyheterna minns man inte', *svt.se*, 26 September 2007, http://www.svt.se/nyheter/inrikes/de-roliga-nyheterna-minns-man-inte (accessed on 22 March 2016).

9 'Medierna i P1', Sveriges Radio, Swedish Public Radio, broadcast on 7 February 2015.

10 'Fatal airliner hull loss accidents', Aviation Safety Network, http://aviation-safety.net/statistics/period/stats.php?cat=A1 (accessed on 22 March 2016).

11 Ed Cumming, 'The scientists with reason to be cheerful', *The Guardian*, 15 November 2015.

12 Martin I. Meltzer, Charisma Y. Atkins, Scott Santibanez, Barbara Knust, Brett W. Petersen, Elizabeth D. Ervin, Stuart T. Nichol, Inger K. Damon, Michael L. Washington, 'Estimating the future number of cases in the Ebola epidemic – Liberia and Sierra Leone, 2014–2015', *Morbidity and Mortality Weekly Report Supplements*, 63, 3 (2014), 1–14.

13 'Predictions with a Purpose', *The Economist*, 7 February 2015.

14 *Strömstads Tidning*, 30 June 2007.

15 Anders Bolling, *Apokalypsens gosiga mörker*. Stockholm: Bonniers, 2009, p. 51.

16 Amos Tversky and Daniel Kahneman, 'Availability: a heuristic for judging frequency and probability', *Cognitive Psychology*, 5, 2 (1973), 207–232.

17 Steven Pinker, 'If everything is getting better, why are people so pessimistic?', *Cato Policy Report*, January/February 2015.

18 Roy F. Baumeister, Ellen Bratslavsky, Catrin Finkenauer and Kathleen D. Vohs, 'Bad is stronger than good', *Review of General Psychology*, 5, 4 (2001), 323–70, p. 323f.

19 Arthur Herman, *The Idea of Decline in Western History*. New York: Free Press, 1997, chap. 1.

20 Lasse Berg, *Ut ur Kalahari: Drömmen om det goda livet*. Stockholm: Ordfront 2014, p. 81.

21 Berg 2014, p. 91.

22 Matt Ridley, 'World outlook: rosy, Europe outlook: awful', *The Times*, 2 January 2013.

23 Eric Jones, *The European Miracle: Environments, Economies and Geopolitics in the History of Europe and Asia*. Cambridge: Cambridge University Press, 1987.

ACKNOWLEDGEMENTS

Several people helped me to turn my ideas about progress into this book. I am very grateful to Jacob Lundberg, who helped me find data series and sources that were difficult to track down. Mattias Bengtsson was – as always – a source of inspiration and support.

My agent Andrew Gordon helped me to develop the whole idea, and supported me throughout. My editor at Oneworld, Alex Christofi, improved the script substantially, and my copyeditor, Kathleen McCully, came up with just the additions and deletions my script needed.

Even though it sometimes feels like it, I am far from the only optimist out there. Since I started writing about globalisation and development in 2001, I have been lucky to come across, meet with and learn from several thinkers who have tirelessly presented the case that humanity solves more problems than it creates, when it gets the freedom to do so. This group includes – but is far from limited to – Ronald Bailey, Lasse Berg, Anders Bolling, Angus Deaton, Robert Fogel, Indur Goklany, Charles Kenny, Deepak Lal, Bjørn Lomborg, Deirdre McCloskey, Joel Mokyr, Steven Pinker, Matt Ridley, Max Roser, Hans Rosling, Michael Shermer and Marian Tupy. And above all, I am indebted to Julian Simon, the grand old man of development optimism.

Their common denominator is not political or even philosophical, but methodological. They look at the whole building rather than just one brick, long data series rather than anecdotes. Of course it's possible to lie with statistics, but it's easier to lie without it.

If you are interested in more data on the world's progress, I urge you to visit and investigate the easily accessible databanks that they and others have compiled, like gapminder.org, humanprogress.org, ourworldindata.org and the World Bank's World Development Indicators.

My deepest debt of gratitude is to my wife and muse, Frida. She gives me both the harmony and the energy needed for my work – and reasons to look forward to the future.

INDEX

abolitionism 146–7
abortion 176–7
acid rain 111
adultery 171–2, 176
Afghanistan 83, 101, 102, 136, 156
Africa 25, 52, 154
  and child labour 193, 195
  and education 133–4
  and HIV/AIDS 59, 60
  and homosexuality 187
  and malnutrition 21, 23–4
  and poverty 79–80, 81
  and slavery 140, 142, 143–4, 145
  and water 38–40
  and women 179
African Americans 162, 163, 167–9
agriculture 13, 14–16, 17–19, 20, 21, 89
  and children 190–1
  and China 27–9
  and land use 22–3, 112
  and water 38
Albert, Prince Consort 32
alcohol 31
algae 15
Algerian War of Independence 94
Amazon rainforest 112
American Civil Liberties Union (ACLU)
    182–3, 185
American Revolution 149
ammonia 14, 15
An Lushan Revolt 95
Ancient Greece 31–2, 44, 84, 140–1, 183
Angell, Norman 103
Angola 21, 83
anti-Semitism 162
antibiotics 2, 50

apartheid 153
Arab Spring 155, 156
Argentina 133
artificial fertilizers 14–15, 18, 22–3, 108
Asal, Victor 170
Asia 67–70, 133, 187, 195
Auld, Hugh 137, 138
Australia 114
Ausubel, Jesse 112
authoritarianism 156

Bacon, Francis 217
bad news 207–12
Bailey, Ronald 205
Bales, Kevin 148–9
Bangladesh 37, 81, 117
Barbary States 143–4
Basu, Kaushik 135
bathing 34, 47
Beccaria, Cesare 93
Bentham, Jeremy 172, 184
Berg, Lasse 68–9, 129, 130, 202–3, 214–15
Berlin Wall 152
Bible, the 84–5, 86, 140, 183
bigotry 188
bio-fuels 125
birth weight 11
Black Death 42
Blackstone, William 184
bloodletting 44, 47
Boko Haram 148
Bolling, Anders 211
Borlaug, Norman 17–19, 23–4
Bosch, Carl 14
Boschwitz, Rudy 23
Bosnia 102

Botswana 27
Brandt, Willy 151
Braudel, Fernand 9, 10, 63
Brazil 153
Britain, *see* Great Britain
Buggery Act (1533) 184
Bure, Anders 132
bureaucracy 216
Burger, Oskar 45
Bush, George W. 187

Caesar, Julius 141
calories 12, 16, 19–20
Cambodia 38
Cameroon 21
Canada 105
cancer 58, 115
cannibalism 8, 10
capital punishment 93–4, 185, 197–8
capitalism 66–7
carbon dioxide 119, 120, 123–4, 127
cardiovascular disease 58
Carter, Jimmy 24
caste system 72–3
Ceauşescu, Nicolae 153
censorship 157
Chad 83
Charlemagne 216
Charta 77: 151
chemical warfare 15
childbirth 4, 48, 49, 53–4, 197
children 11, 12
    and education 133–4
    and labour 189–96
    and malnutrition 22
    and mortality 32, 39–40, 45–6, 51, 53, 56
Chile 132, 153
China 27–9, 112, 200, 216–17
    and child labour 193
    and governance 153, 158
    and homosexuality 187
    and pollution 117, 119
    and poverty 67–8, 69–71, 81
    and slavery 148
    and war 95, 104
    and women 171, 177
chlorine 36–7
cholera 32, 35–6, 45, 55, 197
Churchill, Winston 163
civil rights movement 167–9
civilians 100–1
Clean Air Act (1956) 114
climate change 108, 119–21

Club of Rome 110, 115, 116
codes of honour 91–2
Cold War 99, 182
colonialism 103, 163
combine harvesters 16
communism 25, 26, 28, 102, 151–3, 182
Condorcet, Marquis de 172
Congress of Vienna (1815) 145
contraception 176, 177
crime 93, 207–8, 211
Cronin, Audrey 103
crop failure 7–8, 18
Cuba 132
Czechoslovakia 151, 152

dalits 72–3, 129
Darwin, Charles 45
De Gaulle, Gen Charles 161
'dead zones' 15
death penalty 93–4, 185
Deaton, Angus 12, 52, 61
Declaration of Independence 144–5
Defoe, Daniel 192
deforestation 111–12
dehydration 54–5
democracy 26–7, 104–5, 150–7
Democratic Republic of Congo 26, 81
Dempsey, Gen Martin 2
Denmark 105
diarrhoea 32, 37–8, 54–5
Dickens, Charles 173
dictatorships 150–1, 153, 154, 155, 158
Diderot, Denis 143
discrimination 167–70, 173
Disraeli, Benjamin 36
Divine Comedy (Dante) 183–4
divorce 176
domestic violence 179
Douglass, Frederick 137–8, 139–40, 174
Dublin, Louis 60
dysentery 40

East Germany 152
Ebola 53, 209–10
Economic Freedom of the World 157–8
economics 67–9, 79, 165–6
education 17, 38–9, 135–7, 173, 197; *see also* literacy
Egypt 133, 155, 156
Eisenhower, Dwight D. 168, 182
Eisner, Manuel 90
Ekman, Freddie 208
Elizabeth I, Queen 33, 34

INDEX

energy 123–8
Engels, Friedrich 165–6
Enlightenment, the 4, 13, 66, 93, 184
    and slavery 142–3
    and women 172
environment, the 23–4, 108–12, 113–17
    and climate 119–20
    and energy 123–8
    and poverty 117–19, 120–3
equality 143, 178–9, 188; *see also* inequality
Equatorial Guinea 37
Ethiopia 24
ethnic minorities 161–71
Europe 216, 217–18
extinctions 112–13
extreme poverty 75–8, 79, 80–1

Factory Acts 193
famine 7–10, 13, 14, 17, 25–7, 46, 197
farming, see agriculture
fascism 102
female genital mutilation 179
feminism 173
fertility rates 16–17, 24–5, 56
First World War 14, 15, 99, 104
fish stocks 112
Fitzhugh, George 147
Fleming, Alexander 50
flying toilets 39–40
Flynn Effect 164–5
food 2, 10–14, 13, 16, 17, 19; *see also* famine
Food and Agricultural Organization (FAO) 20–1
forests 111–12
fossil fuels 108
France 9–10, 11–2, 42–3, 63–4, 161–2, 184
Francis, Pope 2
Frederick II, Emperor 32
Free the Slaves 148
freedom 138, 157–9
Friedan, Betty 183
Friedman, Benjamin 166
Friedman, Milton 158–9

Gandhi, Mahatma 168
Garrison, William Lloyd 146
Gates Foundation 52, 125
Gay Pride 185–6
gay rights 181–8
GDP (gross domestic product) 22, 56–7, 64, 67, 74–5
gender gap 178–9
genetically modified crops 23
genocide 101–2

George V, King 104
germ theory 48–9
Germany 114, 152, 183
Gini coefficient 82
globalization 4, 5, 45, 57, 74–5, 82, 218
Glorious Revolution 149
Golden Bull 149
Gorbachev, Mikhail 151
governance 90–1, 92; *see also* democracy
graphene 126
Gray, John 2
Great Ascent 67
Great Britain 12, 114, 145, 192–4
    and homosexuality 184, 185, 186
Great Powers 98–9
Great Smog 107–8, 114
'Great Stink, The' 36
Green Revolution 17–20, 22, 23, 24
greenhouse gases 119
Guan Youjiang 29
Guangdong 70–1

H1N1 virus 59
Haber, Fritz 14, 15
Hagerup, Ulrik 208
Haiti 38, 57, 81, 114
Hans Island 105
happiness 199
Harrington, Sir John 33
Harrison, Dick 140
hate crimes 170
Havel, Václav 151, 152
height 16, 21–2
Helvétius, Claude Adrien 172
Hesiod 213–14
Hilleman, Maurice 54
Hitler, Adolf 94, 95
HIV/AIDS 52–3, 59, 60
Hobbes, Thomas 213
Holocaust, the 102, 170
homicide 85, 89, 90
homosexuality 181–8
Honecker, Erich 152
Hong Kong 67, 70
hookworm 40
human rights 142
human sacrifice 88–9
humanitarianism 93
Hungary 149, 151–2
hunter-gatherers 88
Hutcheson, Francis 143
hygiene 48, 49

India 10, 18–19, 27, 37, 38, 67–9
  and child labour 193, 195
  and governance 151, 154
  and literacy 129–30, 133, 135
  and pollution 117, 119
  and poverty 71–3, 81
  and slavery 145
  and war 104
individualism 92
Industrial Revolution 2, 4, 66, 82
inequality 81–2, 178–9
influenza 58–9
Inglehart, Ronald 166–7
inoculation 47–8
intelligence 164–5
International Labour Organization (ILO) 195–6
International Union for the Conservation of
    Nature 112–13
Iraq 83, 102
irrigation 18, 22, 38
IS 148
Islamists 216
Italy 184, 193

Jang Jin-sung 25–6
Japan 21, 68, 180–1
Japanese Americans 163
Jefferson, Thomas 144, 145, 147
Jenner, Edward 48
Jews 162
Jim Crow laws 162
John, King 149
Johnson, Lyndon B. 169

Kant, Immanuel 201
Karlsson, Stig 68–9, 129, 202–3, 214–15
Kenny, Charles 134
Kenya 39–40
Kibera 39–40
King, Martin Luther, Jr. 168, 181
Klein, Naomi 2
knights 88
knowledge 200–2, 216–18
Korean War 94, 98
Ku Klux Klan 163, 169

land use 22
Las Casas, Bartolomé de 142–3
Latin America 150, 177, 187
law, the 90–1, 92
Lecky, William E. H. 163–4
leprosy 54
Liberia 114

life expectancy 4, 41, 44–7, 49–51, 55, 57–61
  and nutrition 11
  and sanitation 40
Lincoln, Abraham 147
Lipset, Seymour Martin 154
Lister, Joseph Jackson 49
literacy 129–35, 137–8, 198
literature 173
living standards 3–4, 74, 198, 202
Locke, John 149, 164, 192
London 107–8, 110

McCarthy, Joseph 182
Maersk Mc-Kinney Møller (container ship) 123
Magna Carta 149
malaria 52
Malaysia 68
Malleus Maleficarum 87
malnutrition 21, 22, 46
Malthus, Rev Thomas Robert 12–13, 17
Mandela, Nelson 154
Mao Zedong 27, 94, 95, 158
marital rape 177, 179
Marx, Karl 66–7, 165–6
Mattachine Society 182, 185
Mauritania 148
measles 54, 197, 216
media, the 1–2, 4, 207–12
medicine 2, 44, 47
Melville, Herman 173
Mercantilism 65–6
Mexico 17–18, 153, 159
'miasma' 35, 44
microorganisms 48–9
Middle Ages 44, 86–7, 89–90, 171
Middle East 104, 133, 180, 187, 216
milk 16
Mill, John Stuart 172
monarchy 90–1, 92, 149
Mongols 94–5
Montagu, Lady Mary Wortley 47
Montesquieu 93
Mott, Lucretia 174
Moynihan, Daniel Patrick 150–1
Mozambique 21
Mueller, John 97, 100
Muslims 162, 170

Namibia 37
Napoleon Bonaparte 95
Native Americans 163
natural disasters 120, 121, 122
natural resources 115–17

INDEX

Newton, Isaac 202
Nicholas II, Tsar 104
Nicholas V, Pope 141–2
Nichols, Jack 182, 185
Nigeria 21, 81, 102, 159
nitrogen 14–15, 20, 23
North Korea 25–6, 104, 158
nostalgia 213–15
nuclear power 124–5
nuclear weapons 100, 104
nutrition 11–12, 16, 199

Obama, Barack 187
obesity 17
Oeppen, Jim 60
oil spills 111
Omran, Abdel 46
Oneal, John 104–5
oppression 156, 158
Oral Hydration Therapy 54–5
Österlund, Mikael 208
Ottoman Empire 148, 217
ozone layer 110–11

Pakistan 18–19, 37, 102, 104, 117
    and education 135, 136
pandemics 46, 58–9
Pankhurst, Emmeline 175–6
Papua New Guinea 37
Parks, Rosa 168
Pasteur, Louis 49
Pate, Amy 170
Peel, Sir Robert 91
penicillin 50, 51
Pepys, Samuel 43
Peru 21
Pinker, Steven 83–4, 86–7, 89, 94, 98, 165
and psychology 213
Pinochet, Augusto 153
piracy 143–4
plague 41–3, 45, 47
Poland 151
police forces 91
polio 51, 216
pollution 109, 110, 115, 117–18
Popper, Karl 156–7
population rates 12–13, 17, 20–1, 55–6, 94–5
poverty 63–7, 73–9, 80–2, 206–7
    and Africa 79–80
    and China 69–71
    and the environment 117–19, 120–3
    and India 71–3
    and literacy 130, 132, 134

    see also extreme poverty
Prasad, Chandra Bhan 73
prehistory 44
press freedom 157
private schooling 135
protected areas 113
punishment 91, 93–4
Putin, Vladimir 153

racism 161–3, 167–9
Rao, Madhusudan 72–3
religion 84–5, 86, 89–90, 96
    and intolerance 162, 164
    and literacy 131
    and terrorism 102
renewable energy 120
rice 10, 19, 21
Richardson, Samuel 173
Roman Empire 44, 141, 85–6, 183
Romania 153
Roosevelt, Franklin D. 163
Roosevelt, Theodore 163
Roser, Max 209
Rotary Foundation 51
Rousseau, Jean-Jacques 173, 214
Rumbold, Richard 143
Russett, Bruce 104–5
Russia 59–60, 104, 148, 153, 155
    and homosexuality 187
    and women 177
    see also Soviet Union
Rwanda 38, 102

salt 11
same-sex marriage 186–7
sanitation 2, 32–3, 34–40, 47, 49, 197
Sasakawa, Ryoichi 24
Saudi Arabia 177
science 57, 202, 216–17
Second World War 94, 95, 99, 135, 161–2
segregation 167–8, 169
Semmelweis, Ignaz 48
Sen, Amartya 26–7, 150
sewage 33, 34–6, 39, 111
Shermer, Michael 164
Simon, Julian 116
Singapore 67, 70, 154
Singh, Manmohan 71
Sirota, Beate 180–1
slavery 137–8, 139–48, 162, 173, 174, 198
    and modern day 148–9
slums 39–40, 80
smallpox 43–4, 45, 47–8, 51, 197

Smil, Vaclav 14–15
Smith, Adam 66, 143, 165
smog 107–8, 114, 117
Snow, John 35–6
solar power 120, 126, 127
Solidarity 151
Somalia 26, 114, 134
South Africa 153, 154
South Korea 68, 70, 153
Soviet Union 150, 151, 152–3, 187
Spain 98, 142, 154, 155, 162
Spanish flu 59
Spanish Inquisition 87, 184
Spencer, Herbert 201
Sri Lanka 83
Stalin, Joseph 94, 95
Stanton, Elizabeth Cady 174
starvation 7–8, 25–6, 27
Stephens, Alexander 147
Stonewall Inn 185
sub-Saharan Africa, see Africa
Sudan 26, 114
suffrage 150, 175–6, 177–8
superstition 216
surgery 44
Sweden 2, 3, 4, 7–8, 11, 13
    and education 132, 136
    and the environment 114
    and war 97–8
    and women 175
syphilis 45
Syria 83, 102

Taiwan 56, 67, 70, 153, 171
Taliban, the 101, 136
Tanzania 135
technology 114–15, 116–19, 123–4, 129–30,
    200, 216–17
Tegnér, Esaias 98
TerraPower 125
terrorism 83, 102–3, 104, 170
tetanus 51–2
Thailand 134–5, 155
Thames, River 111
Thirty Years' War 94, 97, 162
Thoreau, Henry David 168
Timur Lenk 95
tolerance 164, 165
Tooley, James 135
torture 86–7, 198
trade 13, 69, 96–7, 131, 165–6
    and war 104, 105
Truman, Harry S. 168
tuberculosis 43, 197

Turing, Alan 183
typhoid 31–2, 40

Uncle Tom's Cabin (Stowe) 173
underground railroad 146
undernourishment 9, 12, 20–1, 23
UNICEF 51
United Nations 99
United States of America 104, 162–3
    and civil rights 167–9
    and gay rights 181–3, 185–7
    and slavery 142, 144–5, 146–7
    and women 174–5, 176
unleaded gasoline 119
urbanization 72, 80, 112
Uzbekistan 148

vaccination 48, 49, 51–2, 54, 216
Vaupel, James 60
Ventner, Craig 127
Versailles 33
Vietnam 21, 37, 189, 194
Vietnam War 101
Vindication of the Rights of Women, A
    (Wollstonecraft) 173
violence 83–7, 88, 89–90, 91–2, 197
    and suffrage 175–6
    see also terrorism; war
Voltaire 93, 143, 165
voting rights 150, 174–6, 177–8

Wałęsa, Lech 151
war 19, 25, 83, 94–101, 103–5, 198
water 2, 31–2, 34–40, 47, 49, 197
wealth 56–7, 114, 154–5, 198
Weiner, Eric 208
Wernick, Iddo 112
wheat 18–19
Wilberforce, William 143
wildlife 23, 112–13
Wilhelm II, Kaiser 104
Wilson, Woodrow 163
witchcraft 87–8
Wollstonecraft, Mary 172–3
women 38–9, 60, 87–8
    and education 136, 137
    and rights 150, 171–81, 197
work 12, 67
World Anti-Slavery Convention 174
World Bank 74, 75, 81
World Health Organization (WHO) 32, 51, 52,
    59, 210

Yousafzai, Malala 136